UNDER FIRE

UNDER FIRE

Black Britain in Wartime 1939–45

Stephen Bourne

The
History
Press

First published 2020

The History Press
97 St George's Place, Cheltenham,
Gloucestershire, GL50 3QB
www.thehistorypress.co.uk

British Library Cataloguing in Publication Data.
A catalogue record for this book is available from the British Library.

ISBN 978 0 7509 9435 4

Typesetting and origination by The History Press
Printed and bound in Great Britain by TJ International Ltd.

Contents

Acknowledgements

Keith Howes
Linda Hull
BBC Written Archives Centre
Black Cultural Archives
Commonwealth War Graves Commission
Imperial War Museum (London)
National Archives
West Indian Association for Service Personnel

Author's Note

Under Fire combines some of the stories in two of my previous books: *Mother Country: Britain's Black Community on the Home Front 1939–45* (2010) and *The Motherland Calls: Britain's Black Servicemen and Women 1939–45* (2012), both published by The History Press. It also includes a wealth of new information and personal testimonies, as well as recently discovered photographs, some previously unpublished.

Unlike the previous two books, the material in *Under Fire* has been organised chronologically and thematically. However, the emphasis is still on first-hand testimony from the black Britons who supported the war effort. This comes from published sources and personal interviews by the author.

Over 100 black and mixed-race citizens have been identified by the author in Greater London and across the country in the 1939 Register of England and Wales. This previously unpublished information has been added to the book from www.ancestry.co.uk.

In *Under Fire*, the terms 'black' and 'African Caribbean' refer to Caribbean and British people of African heritage. Other terms, such as 'West Indian', 'negro' and 'coloured' are used in their historical contexts, usually before the 1960s and 1970s, the decades in which the term 'black' came into popular use.

Though every care has been taken, if, through inadvertence or failure to trace the present owners, I have included any copyright material without acknowledgement or permission, I offer my apologies to all concerned.

A Word on Statistics

No official figure exists for the number of people of African descent living in Britain when war was declared on 3 September 1939. Unlike the United States, the ethnicity of British citizens has never been a requirement for a birth certificate, nor was it recorded in the early census returns. Historians do not agree on an accurate figure. In *Black Britannia* (1972), Edward Scobie estimated that in the years from 1914 to 1945 there were 20,000 black people in Britain; in *Wartime: Britain 1939–1945* (2004), Juliet Gardiner claimed that at the outbreak of the Second World War there were no more than 8,000. Professor Hakim Adi suggested to the author that the most realistic estimate for 3 September 1939 was around 15,000, while Jeffrey Green, author of *Black Edwardians* (1998), informed the author that, in his opinion, the figure was at least 40,000.

At the outbreak of war, the largest black communities were to be found in the Butetown (Tiger Bay) area of Cardiff in South Wales, Liverpool and the Canning Town and Custom House area of East London's dockland. In 1935 Nancie Hare's survey of London's black population recorded the presence of 1,500 black seamen, and 250–300 working-class families with West Indian or West African heads of households.[1]

Exact statistics of the number of black men and women from Britain, the Caribbean and Africa who served in the British armed services during the Second World War, or worked for the war effort, are impossible to determine. Ethnicity was not automatically recorded in recruitment papers and no official records of all those working in the many fields of production for the war effort were kept. In 1995, using a variety of Colonial Office sources, Ian Spencer estimated in his contribution to *War Culture* that, of British Caribbeans in military service during the war, 10,270 were from Jamaica, 800 from Trinidad, 417 from British Guiana, and a smaller number, not exceeding 1,000, came from other Caribbean colonies. The majority served in the Royal Air Force (RAF).[2]

In *We Were There*, published in 2002 by the Ministry of Defence, it is claimed:

At the end of the war over three million men [from various parts of the British Empire] were under arms, 2.5 million of them in the Indian Army, over 200,000 from East Africa and 150,000 from West Africa. The RAF also recruited personnel from across the Commonwealth. At first, recruitment concentrated on British subjects of European descent. However, after October 1939 questions of nationality and race were put aside, and all Commonwealth people became eligible to join the RAF on equal terms. By the end of the war over 17,500 such men and women had volunteered to join the RAF, in a variety of roles, and a further 25,000 served in the Royal Indian Air Force.[3]

In 2007, Richard Smith noted in *The Oxford Companion to Black British History*:

From 1941 the British government began to recruit service personnel and skilled workers in the West Indies for service in the United Kingdom. Over 12,000 saw active service in the Royal Air Force … About 600 West Indian women were recruited for the Auxiliary Territorial Service, arriving in Britain in the autumn of 1943. The enlistment of these volunteers was accomplished despite official misgivings and obstruction.[4]

Introduction

I know too well that we would never allow it to be said of us
that when the freedom of the world was at stake we stood aside.

Una Marson (1942)

My interest in documenting the experiences of black citizens on
the home front and in the armed services began with the stories
my adopted Aunt Esther told me. During the war she gave up
her job as a seamstress to do war work. She became a fire watcher
during air raids. While recording my aunt's memories, I began
searching for other stories of black people in wartime Britain,
and I discovered many who have been ignored by historians in
hundreds of books and documentaries produced about Britain
and the Second World War. For example, when I was a teenager
in the 1970s, I borrowed a public library copy of Angus Calder's
The People's War, first published in 1969. Calder mentioned the
existence of a Nigerian air-raid warden in London. So, at an early
age, I was made aware that Aunt Esther was not the only black
person in Britain during the war.

Despite evidence of racial discrimination, black people con-
tributed to the war effort where they could. In Britain, black

people were under fire with the rest of the population in places like Bristol, Cardiff, Liverpool, London and Manchester. Many volunteered as civilian defence workers, such as fire-watchers, air-raid wardens, firemen, stretcher-bearers, first-aid workers and mobile canteen personnel.

These were activities crucial to the home front, but their roles differed from those in the armed services. Factory workers, foresters and nurses were recruited from British colonies in Africa and the Caribbean. Before the Second World War, many in Britain viewed Britain's colonies in Africa and the Caribbean islands as backwaters of the British Empire, but when Britain declared war on Germany, the people of the empire immediately rallied behind the 'mother country' and supported the war effort.

Throughout the empire, black citizens demonstrated their loyalty. Many believed that Britain would give them independence in the post-war years but they recognised that, for this to happen, a battle had to be won between the 'free world' and fascism. This instilled a sense of duty in many citizens of the empire. All citizens in the colonies made important contributions, for example, by volunteering to join the armed services, coming to Britain to work in factories, donating money to pay for planes and tanks, and knitting socks and balaclavas.

This important contribution to the war effort has been ignored by many historians. For some, it may seem strange that black people would support a war alongside white people who did not treat them with equality, but the need to win the war, and avoid a Nazi occupation, outweighed this. Sam King, a Jamaican who joined the Royal Air Force in 1944, said, 'I don't think the British Empire was perfect, but it was better than Nazi Germany.'[1]

In the course of my research, many stories came to light about black servicemen and women, and civilians, confronting racist attitudes in wartime Britain, mainly from the American servicemen who were based there. After the USA entered the war in December 1941, the arrival of around 150,000 African American soldiers from 1942 added to the moral panic of 'racial mixing'.

Black American GIs were segregated from white GIs, but black British citizens and their colonial African and West Indian counterparts served in mixed units.

It was not uncommon for non-American blacks in Britain to find themselves subjected to racist taunts and violence from visiting white American GIs. Conscious of the abuse some black Britons were being subjected to, in 1942 the Colonial Office recommended that they wear a badge, to differentiate them from African Americans and to help protect them. Harold Macmillan, then Under-Secretary of State for the Colonies, supported the idea and suggested 'a little Union Jack to wear in their buttonholes'. Needless to say, the idea came to nothing.[2]

In 2002, when the bestselling author Ken Follett published his wartime espionage thriller *Hornet Flight*, he wasn't expecting criticism for including a black RAF squadron leader in his novel. The squadron leader, Charles Ford, is featured in the prologue with a Caribbean accent, 'overlaid with an Oxbridge drawl'.[3] One of Follett's severest critics was Alan Frampton, who served as a pilot in the RAF between 1942 and 1946. Writing to Follett from his home in Zimbabwe, Frampton said Ford was 'not a credible character' and his inclusion was a 'sop' to black people who may read *Hornet Flight*. An angry Frampton apparently threw down the book in disgust when he came across the Ford character.

In his letter to Follett, Frampton said:

For the life of me I cannot recall ever encountering a black airman of any rank whatsoever during the whole of my service, which included Bomber Command. This may have been a coincidence of course but, in England sixty years ago, blacks were few and far between amongst the population and race was not an issue, unlike today with its attendant racial tensions and extreme sensitivity amounting almost to paranoia. He certainly aroused my indignation, remembering as I do, the real heroes of that period in our history, who were not black. I regard myself as a realist but certainly not an apologist for my race. I have read several of your books and enjoyed them. This one I threw down in disgust.[4]

In his reply to Frampton, dated 19 November 2003, Ken Follett explained:

I'm afraid you're mistaken. The character Charles was inspired by the father of a friend of mine, a Trinidadian who flew eighty sorties as a navigator in the Second World War and reached the rank of squadron leader. He says there were 252 Trinidadians in the RAF, most of them officers. He was the highest ranked during the war, although after the war a few reached wing commander. He received the DFC [Distinguished Flying Cross] and the DSO [Distinguished Service Order]. With true-life heroes as he, there's no need for a 'sop' to black people, really, is there?[5]

The Trinidadian who inspired Follett is Ulric Cross (see Chapters 2 and 14) whose response to Frampton was also recorded:

He must be living in a strange world. I am old enough to have a certain amount of tolerance. People believe what they need to believe. For some reason Frampton needs to believe that. When you know what you have done, what people think is irrelevant.[6]

After 1945, historians of the Second World War, as well as the media (including cinema and television), have portrayed the conflict as one that only involved white men and women. Regrettably, this has continued to be the case, even after the West Indian Association for Service Personnel came into existence in Britain in the 1970s. Since then, the organisation has made great efforts to raise awareness of some of its members' contributions to the Second World War.

As incongruous as Prime Minister Winston Churchill's journey on the London underground in *Darkest Hour* (2017) may have seemed to some cinemagoers, it revealed a united kingdom amongst the people he encountered. His fellow travellers include Marcus Peters (Ade Haastrup), a proud young man of African descent who advises the prime minister that Hitler and the Nazis will never take Piccadilly. This dreamlike sequence is the second time the film's director, Joe Wright, has acknowledged the black presence in Britain in the Second World War. Ten years earlier, in *Atonement* (2007), Wright cast Nonso Anozie, a British actor of Nigerian descent, as a 'tommy' who accompanies Robbie Turner (James McAvoy) to the Dunkirk evacuation of 1940.

Until then, British cinema had barely acknowledged the existence of black servicemen and women from Britain and its colonies during the Second World War. There is no trace of them in any of the 'classic' 1950s war films such as *The Cruel Sea* (1953), *The Dam Busters* (1955), *Reach for the Sky* (1956) and *Dunkirk* (1958). An exception is *Appointment in London* (1953) in which Dirk Bogarde, as a wing commander leading a squadron of Lancaster bombers in wartime, has a brief encounter with a black RAF officer, played by a distinguished-looking but unidentified extra.

In America it has taken decades of integrated casting, 'colour blind' casting, dramatic licence and a better understanding of its history for filmmakers to portray African Americans in Second World War settings. In American cinema there have been some improvements since 1962 when Darryl F. Zanuck's *The Longest Day*, an epic war film about the D-Day landings at Normandy in 1944, failed to acknowledge the contribution of 1,700 African Americans in the first wave establishing the Omaha and Utah beachheads.

With the exception of Joe Wright, British filmmakers are still way behind in acknowledging the presence in the Second World War. Director Christopher Nolan, in the critically acclaimed *Dunkirk* (2017), failed to acknowledge any of the black British soldiers and merchant seamen who were at Dunkirk. Joshua Levine, the historical consultant for *Dunkirk*, in an email to the author (12 November 2019) explained that he did try to identify black British soldiers or personnel at Dunkirk. The closest he came was the London-born Cyril Roberts, who was captured before Dunkirk and remained a prisoner of war (POW) until liberated in 1944. Joshua had read about him in my book, *The Motherland Calls* (2012). However, it is almost certain that other black and mixed-race soldiers, merchant seamen and personnel *were* at Dunkirk, but identifying them is a problem. In which case, why didn't Christopher Nolan use dramatic licence? Many directors do.

When Britain declared war on Germany on 3 September 1939, the colonies rallied to support the war effort. For some, it was an opportunity to show their loyalty to the mother country. For others, especially those who volunteered for the RAF, it was a chance to leave home and have an adventure. For the more progressive-minded in the colonies, the war was seen as a route to post-war decolonisation and independence. Ben Bousquet, co-author of *West Indian Women at War* (1989), said:

> Before the war, in all of the islands of the Caribbean, people were agitating for freedom. With the advent of war, they put aside their protestations, they put aside their battles with the British government, and went to sign on to fight.[7]

In BBC Radio 2's documentary *The Forgotten Volunteers*, the presenter Trevor McDonald commented:

> Altogether over three and a half million black and Asian service personnel helped to win the fight for freedom but, despite the courage and bravery they showed in volunteering to fight, once the war was over, they found that old suspicions returned. Sometimes it's so easy to forget. To all the men and women from the West Indies, Africa and the Indian sub-continent, who volunteered to fight in the first and second world wars, we owe a debt of gratitude and respect.[8]

In 1974, BBC Television screened a ground-breaking historical series called *The Black Man in Britain, 1550–1950*. It was the first British television series to acknowledge that there had been a black community in Britain for over 400 years. The fourth episode in the series, 'Soldiers of the Crown', was one of the first television programmes to acknowledge the contribution made by West Indian servicemen to the Second World War.

Two interviewees stood out, and they summarised the situation in which West Indians found themselves after the declaration of war. They were Ivor Cummings, a black Briton who had been the assistant welfare officer for the Colonial Office, and Dudley Thompson, a Jamaican who had served as a flight lieutenant in the RAF from 1941 until 1945 and with 49 Pathfinders Squadron. He was awarded several decorations. Towards the end of the war Thompson served as a liaison officer with the Colonial Office where he assisted Jamaican ex-servicemen who wanted to settle in London.

In 'Soldiers of the Crown', Cummings explained that he had been denied a commission in the RAF in 1939:

> That rule [in the King's Regulations] excluded all of us. I couldn't join the Royal Air Force because I was not of pure European descent. We were able to get rid of that ridiculous disqualification otherwise we should not have been able to mobilise our volunteers in the way that we did. They wouldn't have qualified for commissions.

When the rule referred to by Cummings was abandoned, it was too late for him to join the RAF because he had accepted a post with the Colonial Office. He said:

> It is not done nowadays to talk about patriotism and the mother country because the Empire does not exist. It *did* exist in 1939 and there was no doubt at all that there was a great feeling of attachment and affection to this country by the colonies, in Africa and particularly in the West Indies.

Cummings commented that one of the most important things that happened to West Indians during the war was the exposure to a different type of government, one that enabled them a certain amount of freedom, a better way of life, and access to a higher standard of education:

> So, when they returned home after the war, they returned to the same government they had left. It was autocratic and people didn't want this. They resented this and the fact that the economic conditions in these places were absolutely appalling. For the returning servicemen and women, the officials, the governors, and others were very tiresome people indeed and didn't know how to deal with those who had been away in the war. After the war I was sent out to the Caribbean and I visited the three major islands, including Jamaica, and I was absolutely appalled. There were no opportunities for these people. The whole thing quite horrified me and I told everyone exactly what I felt about this. It was quite clear to me that this was a watershed. This whole war experience had been a watershed, that there were going to be changes.[9]

For many in the colonies, post-war reform was slow, but the changes they expected eventually came with independence: for example, Ghana (1957), Nigeria (1960), Jamaica (1962), Trinidad and Tobago (1962), Kenya (1963), Guyana (1966) and Barbados (1966).

In 'Soldiers of the Crown', Dudley Thompson described how he felt on arriving in England from Jamaica in 1940:

> As a colonial I would say the effect is confusing in that Jamaica – which you would consider a model colony – always saw the whites as leaders, governors, heads of departments, executives, and so on. You grew up with it. You knew that in the police force, no matter how great you were, you could never get promotion. Those were limitations you accepted. You weren't even militant about it. And then you come to a

country where, for the first time, you see white street sweepers, white bus drivers and other more menial tasks that you never imagined white people did. It was an eye opener. Things were not as you had always expected it to be, and it was a psychologically traumatic situation and more than confusing.

In England during the war, Dudley discovered that it was possible to meet – and make friends with – white people:

You made friends, and you got used to the English way of life. There was a certain amount of courtesy from the English which you did not experience at home and you just adjusted into the English situation which was far from unpleasant. You were accepted as a soldier at a time when soldiers were coming from all parts of the Empire. You were rather proud that you wore a different flash on your shoulder because you saw Poland, France, Australia, Jamaica identified. You were just one of the sections of people whom England was glad to receive as fighting for the general cause.

However, racial conflict was never far away:

You'd find at dance halls there were incidents where they felt black soldiers should not be in that place and sometimes they came from people like the Rhodesian forces who were visiting as well. And you did find occasional cases of friction, so much so that towards the end of the war, liaison officers were created within the Royal Air Force to take care of these situations. I was a liaison officer and from time to time was called to various places where there were disruptions, fights, and ugly incidents that needed smoothing out.

In Jamaica, access to education was restricted, but in wartime Britain, Dudley discovered a whole new world of knowledge opened up to him:

In the colonies there was very limited reading material, most of the books that would be interesting were banned anyway. There was no University. You come to England and find you've got a far more liberal selection of material. You can walk into any library and pursue studies. You can pursue studies of your own country much more widely than you could at home.

Dudley summarised the effect the war had on people from the colonies:

The effect on the armed forces, and the civilians who were munitions workers, was to show that, in England, while you were treated as a normal, average citizen, there were many more opportunities which were open to you there than were open to you at home. You could learn skills, at universities and technical schools, and you became proficient in those skills. Those skills were either non-existent at home or reserved for white people who were ruling you rather than for yourself. So, to a great extent it tremendously increased your self-reliance. The other experience was to show that you were a foreigner and that when you went home you would have to be master in your own house. I would say it increased your sense of national feeling and for the first time you felt that you had to make your own home your own. You also met people from other parts of the Empire who felt similarly, particularly from Africa.[10]

The freedom that the British have enjoyed since 1945 was made possible by the support of the peoples of their former empire. These people made a major contribution to the winning of that freedom. They fought hard for it, and some gave their lives. However, recognition for this support – and the sacrifices made – has been almost non-existent. The historian Ray Costello has offered an explanation for this omission. He said that Britain had been reluctant to show the world that black servicemen and women from Britain and the colonies had played a part in freeing the oppressed, 'because they were afraid that it would feed the desire for independence':

> If black people are shown to have the capacity for bravery it makes them human, heroes even. And heroes should have freedom and independence. Britain did not want that. It was more difficult to conceal our contributions at the end of World War II because of the sheer numbers who fought. The omission of the contribution of blacks to the British armed services is a crime comparable to slavery.[11]

There have been a few exceptions. For example, on 22 June 2017 the first memorial to African and Caribbean servicemen and women was unveiled in Windrush Square, Brixton, and this was made possible by the hard work of Jak Beula, CEO of the Nubian Jak Community Trust.

1939 Register of England and Wales

The 1939 Register provides a snapshot of the civilian population of England and Wales just after the outbreak of the Second World War. It was taken on 29 September 1939 and the information was used to produce identity cards and, once rationing was introduced in January 1940, to issue ration books. Information in the register was also used to administer conscription and the direction of labour, and to monitor and control the movement of the population caused by military mobilisation and mass evacuation.

The following list includes a diverse range of black citizens who are known by the author to have been living in England and Wales at the time the Register was compiled. Additional information, including their country of birth, are noted in italics.

Greater London

Robert W. Adams

b. 18/5/1902 – actor and Air Raid Precautions stretcher bearer
33 Squire's Bridge Road, Sunbury-on-Thames, Middlesex
(aka Robert Adams) (British Guiana, later Guyana) (Died 1965)

Adenrele Ademola
b. 2/1/1916 – probationer nurse
Bassett's Way, Orpington, Kent
(Nigeria, West Africa)

Baba O. Alakija
b. 1/10/1914 – law student
Flat 1, 28 Kensington Church Street, Kensington
(aka Baba Oyeola Alakija) (Nigeria, West Africa) (Joined the RAF)

Amanda C.E. Aldridge
b. 10/3/1866 – teacher of singing
17 Arundel Gardens, Kensington
(aka Amanda Ira Aldridge) (United Kingdom) (Daughter of the Shakespearean actor Ira Aldridge [1807-67]) (Died 1956)

Granville 'Chick' Alexander
b. 25/8/1905 – waiter
6 Howland Street, St Pancras
(Jamaica) (Dancer who worked in civilian defence) (Died 1969)

Rupert Arthurs
b. 15/3/1894 – tailor (master)
26 Benedict Road, Lambeth
(British Honduras, later Belize) (Committee member of the League of Coloured Peoples)

Amy Barbour-James
b. 25/1/1906 – companion help
14 Golf Close, Harrow, Middlesex
(United Kingdom) (Committee member of the League of Coloured Peoples) (Died 1988)

Carl Barriteau
b. 7/2/1914 – musician
5 Marchmont Street, Holborn
(Trinidad) (Died 1998)

Stafford Barton
b. 2/5/1915 – professional boxer and Air Raid Precautions Warden
25 Conway Street, St Pancras
(Jamaica) (Joined RAF and was killed in action in 1943)

Dr Cecil Belfield Clarke
b. 12/4/1894 – Registered Medical Practitioner
Belfield House, Greenhill Park, Great North Road, East Barnet,
Hertfordshire
(Barbados) (Pan-Africanist) (Died 1970)

Rowland W. Beoku-Betts
b. 3/1/1914 – law student
1 South Villas, St Pancras
(West Africa) (President of the West African Students' Union)

Augustus (Joslin) Bingham
b. 5/11/1894 – variety artiste
Flat 4, 9 Charing Cross Road, Westminster
(aka Frisco) (Jamaica) (Nightclub owner in London's West End)

Peter Blackman
b. 28/6/1909 – writer and journalist
61 Glenmore Road, Hampstead
(Barbados) (Pan-African Marxist and scholar, also committee member of the League of Coloured Peoples)

Cyril (McDonald) Blake
b. 27/10/1897 – artiste-musician
10 Rothwell Street, St Pancras
(aka Cyril Blake) (Trinidad) (Died 1951)

Leonard Bradbrook
b. 18/10/1904 – no profession; Air Raid Precautions first-aid stretcher
42 Fitzalan Street, Lambeth
(United Kingdom) (Civilian defence worker) (Died 1991)

Buddy Bradley
b. 25/7/1905 – dance teacher
8 Radnor Place, Paddington
(USA) (Film and stage choreographer) (Died 1972)

Morris Brown
b. 9/4/1909 – hairdresser
22A High Road, Kilburn, Hampstead
(United Kingdom) (Older brother of jazz musician Ray Ellington)

Josephine (Esther) Bruce
b. 29/11/1912 – dress machinist
23 Eli Street, Fulham
(aka Esther Bruce) (United Kingdom) (Seamstress and hospital cleaner who volunteered as a fire watcher) (Died 1994)

Joseph Bruce
b. 25/10/1881 – coach painter
4 Dieppe Street, Fulham
(British Guiana, later Guyana) (Coach painter, father of Josephine E. Bruce) (Died 1941)

Rita (Evelyn) Cann
b. 24/1/1911 – stage artist
143 Fellows Road, Hampstead
(aka Rita Lawrence) (United Kingdom) (Died 2001)

Astley (Campbell) Clerk
b. 2/12/1906 book keeper/accountant
35 Norfolk Place, Paddington
(Jamaica) (died 1961) (born in Spanish Town, Jamaica of Scottish and African descent, Astley came to Britain in 1936 and from 1939-45 he was a Metropolitan Police Reserve Constable in 'D' Division (Marylebone))

Avril Coleridge-Taylor
b. 8/3/1903 – musician and ambulance driver
44A Loudoun Road, St Marylebone
(United Kingdom) (Composer and orchestra conductor, daughter of the composer Samuel Coleridge-Taylor, 1875–1912) (Died 1998)

Joseph Cozier
b. 8/7/1895 – general labourer
27 Catherine Street, West Ham, Essex
(British Guiana, later Guyana) (head of the Cozier family in London's East End)

Frederick Crump
b. 26/1/1902 – artist (travelling)
19 Rochester Road, St Pancras
(aka Freddie Crump) (USA) (Musician – drummer)

Francisco A. Deniz
b. 31/8/1912 – dance band musician
33 Northview, Tufnell Park Road, Islington
(aka Frank Deniz) (United Kingdom) (Died 2005)

Clara E. Deniz
b. 30/9/1911 – dance band musician
(aka Clare Deniz) (United Kingdom) (Wife of Francisco Deniz) (Died 2002)

Joseph W. Deniz
b. 10/9/1913 – musician
196 Westbourne Park Road, Kensington
(aka Joe Deniz) (United Kingdom) (Died 1994)

Yorke de Souza
b. 19/3/1913 – student musician
249 Camden Road, Islington N7
(Jamaica)

Arthur Dibbin
b. 25/10/1901 – travelling trumpet musician
28 Holcombe Road, Tottenham
(United Kingdom)

Evelyn Dove
b. 4/1/1902 – travelling variety artist
23 Roland Way, Kensington
(United Kingdom) (Died 1987)

Rudolph Dunbar
b. 5/4/1907 – journalist
Chiswick Mall Studio
(British Guiana, later Guyana) (Classical musician, orchestra conductor and war correspondent) (Died 1988)

Ekpenyon Ita Ekpenyon
b. 30/12/1898 – artist (films) and Air Raid Precautions Warden
26 Clipstone Street, St Marylebone
(Nigeria, West Africa) (Died 1951)

Frank Essien
b. 10/11/1907 – music hall artist
88 Jermyn Street, Westminster

Titus O. Etiwunmi
b. 26/5/1914 – science student
1 South Villas, St Pancras
(West Africa)

Rudolph Evans
b. 23/2/1897 – musician and entertainer
25 Conway Street, St Pancras
(aka Andre de Dakar) (Panama, South America of Jamaican parents)
(Owner of the Caribbean Club in London's West End 1944–53)
(Died 1987)

Ernest Eytle
b. 18/3/1918 – student
46 Regent Street, St Pancras
(British Guiana, later Guyana) (Cricket commentator)

Nathaniel Fadipe (Akinsemi)
b. 2/10/1893 – lecturer and journalist
23 Regent Square, St Pancras
(Nigeria, West Africa) (Died 1944)

Kier (Farad) Fahmey
b. 1871 – extra, film actor
29 Dieppe Street, Fulham
(North Africa)

Napoleon Florent
b. 8/9/1874 – theatrical artist
19 Camberley House, St Pancras
(St Lucia) (Head of the Florent family, his son Vivian was killed in 1944 while serving in the RAF) (Died 1959)
+ **Josephine Florent** b. 5/7/1910 – typist clerk
+ **Leon Florent** 18/6/1912 – cook
+ **Emile Florent** 1/10/1916 – painter and decorator

Cassandra Foresythe
b. 25/7/1910 – shorthand typist
19 Pierrepoint Road, Acton, Middlesex
(United Kingdom) (Sister of pianist and composer Reginald Foresythe)

Marcus Garvey
b. 17/8/1887 – journalist
53 Talgarth Road, Fulham (home address)
2 Beaumont Crescent, West Kensington (office address)
(Jamaica) (Political activist) (Died 1940)

Winifred Goodare
b. 19/2/1911 – dancer
25 Conway Street, St Pancras
(aka Laureen Goodare) (United Kingdom) (Died 1983)

Phoebe Graham
b. 29/4/1899 – variety artiste (travelling)
11 Grenville Street, St Pancras
(aka Pep Graham) (United Kingdom)

Sidney Graham
b. 25/1/1897 – mercantile marine/ships fireman
24 Crown Street, West Ham, Essex
(Barbados)

Isaac Hatch
b. 21/8/1892 – artist singer
79c Tottenham Court Road, St Pancras
(aka Ike Hatch) (USA) (Nightclub owner) (Died 1961)

Josephine (Lucy) Haywood
b. 16/5/1912 – dancer
61 Great Ormond Street, Holborn
(aka Josephine Woods/Josie Woods) (United Kingdom) (Died 2008)

Louis (Fernando) Henriques
b. 15/6/1916 – student and Auxiliary Fire Service
10 Swiss Terrace, Hampstead
(aka Fernando Henriques) (Jamaica) (Scholar) (Died 1976)

Pauline Henebery
b. 1/4/1914 – unpaid domestic duties
Flat 2 10 South Hill Park Gardens, Hampstead
(aka Pauline Henriques) (Jamaica) (Actress and broadcaster) (Died 1998)

Bert Hicks
b. 4/7/1894 theatrical manager
23 Bruton Lane, City of Westminster
(Trinidad) (Nightclub owner, husband of Adelaide Hall) (Died 1963)
+ **Adelaide Hall** b. 20/10/1901 *(USA) (Entertainer) (Died 1993)*

Marko Hlubi
b. 26/8/1903 student
9 Museum Street, Holborn
(South Africa)

Leslie Hutchinson
b. 7/3/1900 – BBC artiste and variety star
31 Steeles Road, Hampstead
(aka Leslie 'Hutch' Hutchinson) (Grenada) (Died 1969)
+ **Ivan Hutchinson** b. 6/2/1902 – dependent on Leslie Hutchinson
(Grenada) (Brother of Leslie Hutchinson)

Gerald Jennings
b. 13/10/1893 – musician (band leader) + ambulance driver
Flat 2, 21 Southey Road, Lambeth
(aka Al Jennings) (Trinidad) (Died 1980)

Irene B. Jerome
b. 26/1/1891 – unpaid domestic duties
19 Rochester Road, St Pancras
(aka Irene Howe) (Mother of Cyril Lagey and John Lagey, also an actress) (Died 1975)

Kenrick Johnson
b. 10/9/1914 orchestra leader
23 Gloucester Avenue, St Pancras
(aka Ken 'Snakehips' Johnson) (British Guiana, Guyana) (Died 1941)

Amelia E. King
b. 25/6/1917 – box maker
111 John Scurr House, Stepney
(United Kingdom) (died 1995)
+ **Henry King** b. 16/7/1887 greaser Sombardy (ship)
+**Ada A. King** b. 1/9/1916 bag machinist (heavy work)
+ **Frances King** b. 21/4/1920 unpaid domestic duties
+ **Fitzherbert King** b. 18/4/1922 engineering trade

Reverend Israel Kuti
b. 30/4/1891 – minister and professor
1 South Villas, St Pancras
(West Africa)

Cyril J. Lagey
b. 15/1/1912 artist
19 Rochester Road, St Pancras
(United Kingdom) (Musician and comedian) (Died 1999)

John. A. Lagey
b. 20/4/1920 – general labourer
19 Rochester Road, St Pancras
(United Kingdom) (Later known as Johnny Kwango, professional wrestler) (Died 1994)

Alexander Lofton
b. 13/3/1879 – variety artist/vocalist
71 Monkton Street, Lambeth
(USA) (Died 1955)

Benjamin C. MacRae
b. 21/7/1917 ice cream maker
29 Holly Road W4, Brentford and Chiswick, Middlesex
(United Kingdom) (Served in the British Army in WW2) (Died 2001)

Leo D.C. March
b. 19/9/1914 – dental surgeon
26 Hollingbourne Road, Camberwell
(Jamaica)

Ernest Marke
b. 30/8/1901 – medical herbalist
43 Mornington Crescent, St Pancras
(Sierra Leone) (Died 1995)

Una Marson
b. 6/2/1905 – journalist
14 The Mansion, Mill Lane, Hampstead
(Jamaica) (Poet and dramatist who worked as a radio producer and pre-senter for the BBC) (Died 1965)

Emmanuel A. Martins
b. 8/12/1899 – artist
99 Kings Cross Road, St Pancras
(aka Orlando Martins) (Nigeria, West Africa) (Film and stage actor) (Died 1985)

Ras Prince Monolulu
b. 10/10/1881 – tipster, turf adviser
55 Howland Street, St Pancras
(British Guiana, later Guyana) (Died 1965)

Dr Harold A. Moody

b. 8/10/1882 – medical practitioner

164 Queens Road, Camberwell

(Jamaica) (Community leader, president of the LCP and head of the Moody family) (Died 1947)

+ **Dr Christine Olive Moody** b. 12/5/1914 – medical practitioner

+ **Harold Ernest A Moody** b. 1/11/1915 – student

+ **Charles A Murcott Moody (aka Charles 'Joe' Moody)**
b. 15/4/1917 – student

John Nit

b. 27/8/1907 – professional dancer and Air Raid Precautions Warden

41 Howland Street, St Pancras

(USA)

Ladipo Odunsi

b. 14.1.1911 – law student

1 South Villas, St Pancras

(West Africa)

George Padmore

b. 28/6/1900 – author and working journalist

23 Cranleigh House, St Pancras

(aka Malcolm Nurse) (Trinidad) (Pan-Africanist and member of the Communist Party) (Died 1959)

Uriel Porter

b. 5/5/1911 – singer

34 Mornington Crescent, St Pancras

(Jamaica) (Died 1985)

Harry Quashie
b. 3/12/1899 – artist
4 Rothwell Street, St Pancras
(Ghana) (Film and stage actor) (Died 1982)

George A. Roberts
b. 1/8/1891 – exhibition attendant and Auxiliary Fire Service
29E Lewis Trust Dwellings, Warner Road, Camberwell
(Trinidad) (Committee member of the League of Coloured Peoples)
(Died 1970)

Edmundo Ros
b. 9/12//1910 – musician artiste
77 Linden Gardens, Kensington
(Trinidad) (Died 2011)

Winifred Scott
b. 29/7/1917 – probationer nurse
26 Selbourne Road, Chiselhurst and Sidcup
(United Kingdom)

Cornelia Estelle Smith
b. 29/4/1875 – variety and film artist
14 Brook Drive, Lambeth
(aka Connie Smith) (USA) (Died 1970)

Norris Smith
b. 18/2/1883 – music hall artist
88 Jermyn Street, Westminster
(USA) (Died 1959)

Ladipo Solanke
b. 3/3/1893 – barrister at law
1 South Villas, St Pancras
(Nigeria, West Africa) (Founder of the West African Students' Union)
(Died 1958)

Opeolu 'Olu' Solanke
b. 12/4/1910 – unpaid domestic duties
1 South Villas, St Pancras
(Nigeria, West Africa) (Wife of Ladipo Solanke)

James M. Solomon
b. 3/6/1880 – variety artist
101 Walton Street, Chelsea
(West Indian-born film and stage actor) (Died 1940)

Fela Sowande
b. 29/5/1905 – dance pianist
20 Northview, Tufnell Park Road, Islington
(Nigeria, West Africa) (Musician and composer) (Died 1987)

Louis Stephenson
b. 2/6/1907 – musician
249 Camden Road, Islington N7
(Jamaica)

Rita (Kathleen) Stevens
b. 2/10/1909 – artist on tour
Hillmarton Road, Islington
(United Kingdom)

Monteith Tyree
b. 19/7/1902 musician
155 Brixton Road, Lambeth
(aka Monty Tyree) (United Kingdom) (Son of African American singer and guitarist Monteith Tyree)

Mathias Vroom
b. 27/3/1898 – artist
16 Mornington Crescent, Islington
(West Africa)
+ **Frances Vroom** b. 15/2/1904 – artist
(United Kingdom)

Edward Henry Wallace
b. 16/11/1871 – vocalist and travelling instrumentalist
16 Kennington Road, Lambeth
(USA) (Died 1965)

Otto L. Wallen
b. 31/1/1896 – medical practitioner
48 Coram Street, Holborn
(Trinidad)

Elisabeth Welch
b. 27/2/1909 – theatre artist
1 Cottage Walk, Chelsea
(USA) (Died 2003)

David Wilkins
b. 25/9/1914 – musician
49 Sussex Gardens, Paddington
(aka Dave Wilkins) (Barbados) (Died 1990)

Charles Wood
b. 18/8/1914 – music hall artist
14 Maple Street, St Pancras
(United Kingdom) (Brother of Josephine (Lucy) Haywood (see above))

Henry P. Zulamkah
b. 15/6/1887 – showman performer
Hillmarton Road, Islington

Outside Greater London

Bolaji O. Alakija
b. 15/11/1902 – medical student
Broadmoor Asylum, Easthampstead, Berkshire

Richard Barr
b. 10/7/1881 – general builders' labourer
76 Main Street, Penzance, Cornwall
(Of African descent) (Served in First World War) (Died 1955)
+ **Richard Barr** b. 10/5/1913 – lorry driver heavy goods
(United Kingdom) (Served in RAF, killed in action)
+ **William Barr** b. 3/10/1928 – at school
(United Kingdom)

Edward Bovell
b. 2/6/1866 – ship's cook and steward (retired)
26 Sophia Street, Cardiff, Glamorganshire
(Barbados) (Volunteered for Air Raid Precautions) (Died 1961)

John Harrison Cockle
b. 18/12/1912 merchant seaman (mercantile marine war service)
24 Trelander South, Truro, Cornwall
(United Kingdom)

Hiawatha (Bryan) Coleridge-Taylor
b.13/10/1900 – copyright music agent
Hill Top, Sussex
(United Kingdom) (Son of the composer Samuel Coleridge-Taylor, 1875–1912) (Died 1980)

Learie Constantine
b. 21/9/1902 – professional cricketer
3 Meredith Street, Nelson, Lancashire
(Trinidad) (Died 1971)
+ Norma Constantine
b. 23/11/1905 – unpaid domestic duties
(Trinidad)

George D. Ekarte
b. 1/1/1904 – pastor and missioner
122-124 Hill Street, Liverpool, Lancashire
(aka Daniels Ekarte) (West Africa) (Died 1964)

Rufus E. Fennell
b. 7/11/1887 – author, playwright and market salesman
Wendon Dene, Bardney, Welton, Lincolnshire
(USA) (Died 1974)

Ellis (Thompson) Jackson
b. 5/5/1869 – music hall artist
112 The Driveway, Canvey Island, Essex
(USA) (Died 1989)

Albert James
b. 11/4/1888 – iron dresser (iron foundry)
142 Selborne Street, Liverpool
(United Kingdom)

Sarah Francisco
b. 28/7/1894 – professional singer (theatre)
33 Loudoun Square, Cardiff
(aka Sadie Hopkins) (United Kingdom)

Turner Layton
2/7/1894 music hall artist
Castle Hotel, Norwich
(USA)(Died 1978)

Teresa Link
b. 2/12/1913 – variety artiste
2 Evelyn Street, Cardiff, Glamorganshire, Wales
(United Kingdom)

Geoffrey Love
b. 4/9/1917 – musician instrumentalist and variety artist
Hastings, Sussex
(aka Geoff Love) (United Kingdom) (Died 1991)

William A. Miller
b. 15/7/1890 – electrical wireman and Air Raid Precautions Warden
10 East Street, Plymouth, Devon
(United Kingdom) (Died 1970)

Charles Minto
b. 18/7/1893 – cook
16 Limewood Road, Tynemouth, Northumberland
(aka Charles Udor) (Nigeria, West Africa) (Community leader in Tyneside)

John C. Payne
b. 26/6/1872 – private means
Liskeard, Cornwall
(USA) (Retired singer) (Died 1952)

John Pervoe
b. 25/1/1859 – retired boarding house keeper
8 Peel Street, Cardiff, Glamorganshire, Wales
(Nova Scotia, Canada) (Parents were West Indian) (Died 1943)
+ **Edith (Maud) Bryan** b. 15/6/1890 – unpaid domestic duties
(United Kingdom) (Daughter of John Pervoe) (Died 1979)

Basil Rodgers
b. 5/9/1900 – gardener
Evesbro, 2 Loring Road, Salcombe, Devon
(United Kingdom) (Also a concert singer) (Died 1983)

Beatrice Sinclair
b. 1/12/1909 – unpaid domestic duties
19 Frances Street, Cardiff
(United Kingdom)

Ida Mary Smith
b. 9/12/1908 – unpaid domestic duties
Perdue, Close Lane, Alsager, Cheshire
(aka Ida Shepley) (United Kingdom) (Singer who joined the Entertainments National Service Association [ENSA]) (Died 1975)
+ **Cyril Humphrey** b. 17/5/1912 – bullion dealer
(United Kingdom) (Brother of Ida Mary Smith)

Edward Peter Whaley
b. 22/9/1884 – music hall artist
12 Wyndham Square, Plymouth, Devon
(aka Eddie Whaley) (USA) (member of a double-act, Scott & Whaley) (Died 1960)
+ **Harry Scott** b. 18/11/1879 – music hall artist
(USA) (Died 1947)

Grace Wilkie
b. 24/1/1918 – unpaid household duties
40 Berkley Street, Liverpool, Lancashire
(United Kingdom)

1

3 September 1939

Following Adolf Hitler's rise to power in Germany in 1933, the shadow of war hung over Europe. For British civilians across the empire, the war really began on 1 September 1939, the morning Hitler's troops marched into Poland. Following the toll of Big Ben, at 11.15 a.m. on Sunday, 3 September 1939, Prime Minister Neville Chamberlain made a BBC Radio broadcast to the nation. After months of uncertainty, Chamberlain informed the nation that Britain had declared war on Germany.

Those who heard the voice of Chamberlain on that fateful morning never forgot their feelings of horror and dread of the unknown. Within minutes, air-raid sirens could be heard, and some thought that death and destruction was imminent. It was a false alarm. There would be no air raids until the following summer.

Jamaican-born Pauline Henebery and her English husband had just moved into a flat in Hampstead when they heard Chamberlain's famous speech. Pauline recalled, 'And then the air-raid warning sounded immediately after Chamberlain's speech, and we thought let's get out. The flat was right on the edge of the Heath, so we climbed up Parliament Hill.'[1] From the top of

Parliament Hill, the Heneberys watched barrage balloons rising across London:

> It was almost magical, although the implications were frightening. But it was just amazing to see it, to see these great grey shapes rising up. They had a children's story-book image about them and they were covering the whole – or so it looked – the whole of London. It was not really an air-raid warning. I think it was probably done to alert people to the importance of what had happened, and I don't think that any of us at that time really believed the Germans were flying over London and were going to attack us then and there … In a funny sort of way, we really didn't have any knowledge of what was going to happen, so I don't think we were frightened. There was a little bit of what I call sick excitement.[2]

Pauline described herself as a 'comfortably off' young housewife when the war started. She was married to Geoffrey Henebery, an insurance clerk, and they had a 2-year-old daughter. Pauline had been born in Jamaica. In 1919, when she was 5 years old, she settled with her middle-class family in St John's Wood, an affluent part of north London. Pauline's father, Cyril Henriques, was a successful import and export merchant and wanted his six children to have an English education. Pauline described him as 'a most interesting man. He was well educated, cultured and had a passion for reading, music and the theatre.'[3]

Pauline's parents had just returned to Jamaica and, when the threat of war became a reality, they immediately wrote to her and asked her to leave Britain and stay with them but, Pauline said:

> I felt that my roots were here. It was where I'd spent all my childhood from the age of five. It was where my friends were, and most of the family – one of my two brothers and both my sisters were living in England. And now my husband was here.[4]

Pauline didn't expect to join up:

> In those days when you married and had children you stayed
> at home. I took it for granted this was my role. In any case, at
> the beginning of the war, I was a pacifist and didn't entertain
> any thoughts of joining up.[5]

When Britain declared war on Germany, American visitors and
expatriates who had settled there were advised by their government to return home, but the American-born singer and
entertainer Adelaide Hall decided to stay. She took a great risk,
with the threat of a German invasion and possible air raids.
Adelaide explained that she remained in Britain because she was
married to a British subject and refused to leave him. Her husband, Bert Hicks, was a Trinidadian. Bert tried to persuade his
wife to return home to her mother in New York but, she said, 'I
wanted to stay because I liked England and the people here were
very good to me. They were very kind. I didn't want to desert
them, or my husband. So, I stayed.'[6]

Adelaide and Bert had only recently taken over a West End
nightclub called the Old Florida, which they relaunched as the
New Florida. It was situated in Bruton Mews, off Conduit Street,
close to Bond Street and Berkeley Square. Adelaide had a small flat
above the club, and Bert had an office. Though primarily a private
membership club for the armed services, Adelaide's appearances
in the New Florida's late-night revues attracted many celebrities
of the day as well as members of the royal family. The Nigerian
pianist and composer Fela Sowande was employed as Adelaide's
accompanist. Fela was quiet and unassuming. Adelaide said, 'He
wore spectacles, and Bert said he looked more like a medical student than a musician!'[7]

Joseph Bruce, born in British Guiana (later Guyana), a British
colony in South America, had been a merchant seaman. He settled in London in the Edwardian era. He earned a living as a
labourer, and then as a coach painter. After making his home in

Fulham, West London, he married Edith Brooks. Their mixed-race daughter Esther was born in 1912. The Bruce family integrated into the tightknit working-class community of Dieppe Street, near North End Road but, in 1918, Joseph's wife died. He raised Esther on his own.

After leaving school, Esther worked as a seamstress. For several years she had a job at the famous department store, Barkers of Kensington, until a new manager took over. He promptly sacked her for being 'coloured'. Following this distressing experience, Mary Coy Taylor, who ran her own dressmaking business in her house in Markham Square, Chelsea, offered Esther a job. Esther described her as kind and generous.

At the outbreak of war, Joseph tried to persuade Esther to leave Britain, and make the journey to British Guiana, to live with his mother. She refused. Esther was a young woman of 26 and had a mind of her own. She refused to leave her father and the community in which she had been raised. Although she had been corresponding with her grandmother in British Guiana, Esther had never met her. Esther looked upon the Fulham community in which she lived as her extended family.

One of the first black people to be seen in British cinemas in wartime was a popular figure in the 1920s and 1930s. This was the flamboyant racing tipster – and showman – Ras Prince Monolulu. Almost everyone in Britain heard about him, and he couldn't be mistaken, with his headdress of ostrich feathers, multicoloured cloak and gaiters, tartan shawl wrapped around his waist, a huge shooting stick-cum-umbrella in his hand, and a lion-claw necklace round his neck. Then there was his catch-phrase, 'I gotta horse!', which he shouted at the top of his voice.

In the 1930s Monolulu, the entertainer Leslie 'Hutch' Hutchinson and singer and actor Paul Robeson were among the most famous black men in Britain. One week after the outbreak of war, Monolulu was seen in *London Carries On*, a British Movietone News newsreel dated 11 September 1939. The film's commentator, Leslie Mitchell, informed cinema audiences that

Monolulu has 'evidently adapted himself to the new conditions'. Monolulu is seen amongst a London crowd, encouraging the use of gas masks, and adapting his famous catchphrase, 'I gotta gas mask to protect you!' He added, 'Are we afraid of Hitler? Are we downhearted?' To which the cheerful crowd replied, 'No!' The film is in keeping with the spirit of the times. War had just been declared, and morale boosting propaganda was needed. Monolulu was a reassuring figure.

Esther Bruce didn't like her gas mask:

I hated mine. It smelled of rubber. I only wore mine once. In the war we had the blackout and you couldn't see each other in the street so if you walked into someone you'd say: 'Sorry, mate'. Sometimes it was only a lamp post but you still said sorry! And then you'd laugh at yourself and say: 'What's the matter with me? It was only a lamp post!'[8]

The war had hardly started when Adelaide Hall began entertaining the troops. On 17 October 1939 she starred in a variety concert at the RAF station in Hendon. Other artistes on the bill included the famous comedy actor Will Hay, who introduced the show.

The BBC broadcast part of the show, the very first wartime concert broadcast live on the air. Part of the concert, including Adelaide, was filmed by British Paramount News, and this newsreel has survived in the Imperial War Museum's collection. In the film, Adelaide can be glimpsed enjoying herself onstage performing a singalong number with the troops. It's called 'I'm Sending You the Siegfried Line (to Hang Your Washing On)', a variation on the more famous wartime favourite, 'We're Gonna Hang Out the Washing on the Siegfried Line'.

On 26 October 1939, a matter of a few weeks or so after the war started, Earl Cameron, a young sailor from Bermuda, arrived at Woolwich Docks in the East End of London. Later in the war, Earl left the navy, settled in London and became a professional actor, but he never forgot his first impression of the metropolis:

At night-time, everything was blacked out. We were issued gas masks and forced to carry them with us at all times. To be honest, I don't think they would have been of much protection if a full-scale gas attack actually happened from the Germans. England, at that time, was barely prepared for a full attack from the enemy. The Germans soon took a large part of Europe, including Holland, France and Belgium. This was, of course, before the great Winston Churchill had come on the scene. Neville Chamberlain, the Prime Minister, appeared to have had no idea how to handle Adolf Hitler. I can recall one of the evening newspaper's headlines in early December saying 'Peace by Christmas'. Little did one realise that the world was facing more than five years of the most terrible war that civilisation would ever encounter.[9]

2

The Colour Bar

In 1939, black British citizens had more social freedom than African Americans. Unlike in America, mixed marriages had not been outlawed in Britain. In most social situations, black and white could mix freely. For example, there was no enforced racial segregation on buses or in cinemas as there was in the United States. However, racist attitudes existed in all walks of life, and there were many places, such as housing, hotels, clubs, public houses and restaurants, that operated what was then known as the 'colour bar'. So, there was nothing in law to prevent landlords and landladies from barring black tenants, hotel managers from refusing black guests or public houses from excluding black customers. Such practices were not outlawed until the 1960s.

In 1952, when he reflected on his trip to Britain in the 1940s, the African American journalist Roi Ottley observed:

> In brief, there is nothing in law to prevent Negroes from being first-class British citizens. But they do meet discrimination … as the English draw social lines sharply, even indeed refusing accommodations to lower-class white persons. This is English

snobbery – but a formidable reality to which all classes seem to genuflect.[1]

In 1939, the colour bar also existed in the armed services, but this hadn't always been the case. For example, in the First World War a number of black British men were recruited into various army regiments and some, such as Walter Tull (1888–1918), were promoted. In 1915, the Jamaican pilot William Robinson Clarke (1895–1981) joined the Royal Flying Corps (which later became the Royal Air Force) and he was decorated for his bravery and heroism.[2]

After the First World War, the RAF stopped recruiting non-whites. For example, in 1938, Sydney Kennard, the son of an English doctor and his black wife, had applied to join the RAF but he had been refused entry, even though he had been to America to study aviation and was given his pilot's licence. He paid his way back to England, with the intention of joining up, but they wouldn't accept him.

In the late 1930s, the British Army's adjutant general, Sir Robert Gordon-Finlayson, had recommended to the Army Council that commissions for all the armed services should be reserved for British subjects of British parents of European descent. However, when it became law, the Colonial Office was given the job of accommodating black Britons, including those from African and Caribbean colonies, who wished to fight the Nazis when the war broke out. They wrote to the War Office to have the law changed. The War Office replied that it was considering this 'thorny problem', but British policy towards colonial volunteers remained equivocal. A Foreign Office memo dispatched to colonial governors stated, 'We must keep up the fiction of there being no colour bar. Only those with special qualifications are likely to be accepted.'[3]

Whitehall's reluctance to accept volunteers of African heritage dated back to the First World War but, as the Second World War escalated, Britain turned once more to its black subjects, including those in the Caribbean and other colonies, for support.

Meanwhile, when the war broke out, Charles Arundel Moody, aged 22, known as 'Joe' to his family and friends, qualified for basic training as an officer in the British Army. With a public-school education at Alleyn's School in Dulwich, South London, Joe went to a recruiting office in Whitehall for an interview but was dismayed when he was turned away on the grounds that officers in the British Army had to be of 'pure European descent'.

Joe had a Jamaican father and an English mother. However, Joe's father, Dr Harold Moody, was no ordinary Jamaican. Dr Moody had settled in Britain in the Edwardian era and by 1939 was a highly respected community leader. He had been fighting the colour bar since his arrival here in 1904. The League of Coloured Peoples (LCP), which he had founded in 1931, had quickly established itself as the most influential organisation campaigning for the rights of black people in interwar Britain.

When Joe informed his father about his rejection from the army, an angry Dr Moody fought back. He contacted the Colonial Office and made an appointment with one of the undersecretaries. That meeting started the process which led to the Army Act being changed. Dr Moody and other members of the LCP joined forces with the International African Service Bureau (IASB) and the West African Students' Union (WASU) to lobby the government. Consequently, on 19 October 1939, the Colonial Office issued the following statement, 'British subjects from the colonies and British protected persons in this country, including those who are not of European descent, are now eligible for emergency commissions in His Majesty's Forces'. But Dr Moody remained unsatisfied. 'We are thankful for this,' he said, 'but we do not want it only for the duration of the war. We want it for all time. If the principle is accepted now, surely it must be acceptable all the time.'[4] Dr Moody and the LCP emphasised that they would not be satisfied by concessions in individual cases. He said:

May I make myself and the position of the League quite clear?
We are not seeking for specialist treatment in every case. We
are merely seeking to establish our spiritual, cultural and
mental equality, as members of the British Empire, with every
other member of the Empire and to embody the term 'British
Citizen' with some meaning and some reality as far as we are
concerned. We claim the right to that freedom, which is the
cherished possession of every Englishman and that no discrimination whatsoever should be made against us, except on the
grounds of character and qualification. We are proud of our
heritage and do not want to be subjected to any experience,
which will in any way tend to rob us of that pride or which
will cast a slur thereupon.[5]

Soon afterwards, the army began to make exceptions.
Commissions as lieutenants were granted to Dr Otto Wallen of
Trinidad and Dr A. Marsh of Jamaica in the Royal Army Medical
Corps. Joe Moody was sent to Dunbar in Scotland where he
joined an officer-cadet training unit:

> I went through four months of intense training where, because
> I was literally a guinea pig, I had to be very careful and mind
> my ps and qs and really perform outstandingly. I didn't get
> thrown out so I guess they thought I could make it.[6]

On the completion of his training, Joe was commissioned into
the Queen's Own Royal West Kent Regiment. In addition to
Joe, four more of Dr Harold Moody's six children received army
or Royal Air Force commissions during the war: Ronald served
in the RAF; Christine and Harold both qualified as doctors and,
after a short period in practice with their father at Peckham, they
joined the Royal Army Medical Corps and became captain and
major respectively. Dr Moody's youngest son, Garth, became a
pilot-cadet in the RAF.

As the war intensified, and with inadequate manpower available, Britain turned to its colonies and appealed to both white

and black colonial subjects to bolster military ranks. The need for black recruits became more urgent in 1940 after the Fall of France and the loss of British troops at Dunkirk and then the Battle of Britain. There was uneasiness about recruiting black colonials because a feeling of nationalism had grown in the colonies in the 1930s; yet most colonial servicemen joined up because they remained loyal to the mother country as they had done in the past, such as when they gave support during the First World War.

By the end of 1940, the RAF began to recruit men from Britain's West African and Caribbean colonies. One of them was the Trinidadian Ulric Cross. In 1990, when he was featured on BBC Television in the discussion programme *Hear-Say*, he explained why he joined, 'I was young, adventurous and idealistic'. He said he hated 'the frustrations and the stultifying nature of colonial society, particularly in a very small country', but added that 'the whole idea of being a member of the Royal Air Force was romantic'. Hitler's treatment of the Jews was also 'an important element', but for Ulric the romantic view of the RAF had been with him since his schooldays. He explained that, at the age of 14, he had written his name as 'Flight Lieutenant P.N.U. Cross DFC' in the flyleaves of two of his school books. 'To me that was the height of anybody's ambition, to be a Flight Lieutenant in the Royal Air Force and to get the DFC. Most of my friends thought I was mad.'[7]

On 17 October 1939 the *Daily Herald* reported that three black Air Raid Precautions workers (stretcher bearers) in the central London borough of Paddington had resigned because of racist attitudes shown towards them. The Reverend E.N. Jones, a Sierra Leonean who was also known as Lamina Sankoh, alleged that he was 'dismissed' because of his complaints about racism. The *Daily Herald* described Mr Jones as an 'Anglican clergyman, M.A. of Durham and Oxford graduate'. He was also a leading member of WASU.

The union took up the case and, after protesting to the Paddington Borough Council, their secretary, Ladipo Solanke told the *Herald* that he had written to the Home Secretary and several

Members of Parliament about the situation. WASU highlighted the evil of the colour bar during wartime, 'especially at a time when colonial subjects were being asked to risk their lives in defence of the Empire'.[8] The Paddington Air Raid Precautions (ARP) refuted the allegations, 'It is not true there is any colour prejudice'.

Lilian Bailey, born in the Toxteth Park area of Liverpool, was the mixed-race daughter of Marcus Bailey, a merchant seaman who came from Barbados. As a young woman in the 1930s Lilian made many attempts to find a job, but often she faced racism at job interviews. She said, 'You sit there looking very stoic, pretending you don't care, wishing you were out of it. Nobody would employ me. I realised I had a problem with colour.'[9]

Eventually Lilian found employment in domestic service but, when the war broke out, she was determined to support the war effort. She began at the age of 21 in September 1939 with the Navy, Army and Air Force Institutes (NAAFI). This was an organisation that had been set up in 1921 to provide recreational establishments needed by the British armed forces.

Posted to the NAAFI in Catterick Camp, near Richmond in North Yorkshire, the friendly and outgoing Lilian enjoyed canteen life, where she made many friends. Seven weeks later, she was asked to leave. Her father's Barbadian background had been discovered by an official in London. For several weeks her supervisor avoided informing her of this decision, but eventually had to tell her the truth and release her. Lilian later explained this came about because of the hysteria in Britain in the early months of the war 'when anyone who looked a bit foreign or different was treated with suspicion'.[10]

Reluctantly, Lilian returned to domestic service, but she felt embarrassed when a group of soldiers at a gun post expressed surprise that she was not doing war work. 'How could I tell them that a coloured Briton was not acceptable, even in the humble NAAFI?'[11]

In June 1939, the Ministry of Agriculture recreated the Women's Land Army (WLA) – a throwback to the First

World War. By August that year, the WLA had 30,000 recruits. However, when Amelia King, a young mixed-race woman, volunteered to join, she was turned down because of her colour. It was an act of racism that led to coverage in the popular press and caused outrage by members of the British public who read the story.

Amelia was born in Limehouse in the East End of London. Her father, Henry King, from British Guiana, was serving in the merchant navy. Later, her younger brothers, Frances and Fitzherbert, both served in the Royal Navy during the Second World War. So, it is evident that Amelia and her brothers shared a strong moral commitment to fighting the good fight and serving their king and country.

In 1943, at the age of 26, Amelia applied to the Essex County Committee to join the WLA. She was interviewed at their offices in Oxford Street in London's West End, but a female official told her that there would be difficulties in finding her a placement because farmers would object to her 'colour' and some of the locals with whom she might have been billeted would also object. Amelia was then sent to meet an official at the Stratford Labour Exchange where she was informed that the Essex County Committee had rejected her for the WLA. No reason was given, and Amelia was offered a job in a munitions factory. Amelia declined the offer and argued that, if her 'colour' wasn't good enough for the WLA, then it wasn't good enough for the munitions factory.

Amelia was a proud and defiant woman who fought back. It must have been a difficult decision to make a stand in wartime, when everyone was being encouraged to 'pull together' for the war effort. Yet Amelia persisted. After a second attempt to volunteer for the WLA and a second refusal, she took her case to her Member of Parliament, Walter 'Stoker' Edwards, an ex-dockworker and Labour Party member. There was press coverage and Amelia made the front page of the *Daily Mirror* on 24 September 1943, which drew attention to Amelia's predicament.

When Walter Edwards confronted the House of Commons with Amelia's story, the Conservative Minister of Agriculture, Robert Hudson, made the following excuse:

> Careful enquiry has been made into the possibility of finding employment and a billet for Miss King, but when it became apparent that this was likely to prove extremely difficult, she was advised to volunteer for other war work where her services could be more speedily utilised.

Edwards responded:

> In view of the insult that has been passed to this girl and to her father and brother, both of whom are doing valuable war work, cannot the Minister do something about the farmers who are responsible for this position?

Hudson replied, 'I do not employ members of the Women's Land Army. It is not like other Women's Services.' When questioned, he said that he did not endorse the colour bar. Another MP told Hudson that 'the world listens to matters of this kind, which affect the integrity of the British people', but Hudson made no reply.[12]

The racism experienced by Amelia King aroused feelings of anger in many British people. In one poll carried out by the public opinion organisation, Mass Observation, 49 per cent of the 62 per cent who had heard about Amelia 'strongly disapproved' of her treatment while a further 12 per cent 'disapproved'. A rider was added that said even those who did not entirely believe in race equality were against this particular case of prejudice which was regarded as detrimental to the war effort.[13]

Although no record has come to light of Amelia's point of view, there was a farmer called Alfred Roberts, of Fareham, Hampshire, who shed some light on what happened to her. He explained in his unpublished memoir that, in 1943, when he read about

Amelia in the newspapers, he offered her a job on his farm. Amelia was thrilled with Mr Roberts' offer of work, but she insisted on going through the official channels. Amelia also requested formal membership of the WLA. On 9 October 1943, the *Daily Express* reported that Amelia's request had been accepted and she took up her position on Mr Roberts' farm with twenty-five other young women. She was also offered accommodation by at least four villagers who lived near the farm.[14]

3

Dr Harold Moody

In the 1930s and 1940s, Dr Harold Moody was more than just a popular family doctor. He was an ambassador for Britain's black community and an important figurehead who campaigned to improve the situation for black people in Britain, especially during the Second World War. In 1972, Edward Scobie described Moody in his book *Black Britannia* as a man whose leadership and strength of character won the respect of English people and carried the LCP through many difficult periods, gaining it the respect and admiration of white and black alike. Scobie added that Dr Moody's counterpart could be seen in the charismatic African American leader, Dr Martin Luther King Jr:

> They were both devout men with an innate love of mankind and the profound belief that in the end, good will prevail. To many extremists among the Africans and West Indians in Britain in the thirties, Dr Moody was looked upon as something of an Uncle Tom – much as Black Power supporters and some extremists looked upon Dr King in his last years. This in no way detracts from the good that Dr Moody and the League

of Coloured Peoples [LCP] did for the thousands of blacks living in Britain between the two world wars.[1]

As well as being a doctor, Harold Moody was driven by his Christian faith to be active in his community in South London's Peckham and Camberwell. He became involved with church affairs as soon as he arrived in Britain. In his community, he helped to run the Camberwell Green Congregational Church in Wren Road, where he was a deacon and lay preacher. He often used church pulpits to put across his views of racial tolerance. English dignitaries attended these services, the highlight being the singing of spirituals.

Like most settlers of African descent, Dr Moody became frustrated with the racial discrimination he encountered in Britain. He helped many black people who came to him in distress. They told him about the difficulties they faced in trying to find work or somewhere to live. Sometimes Dr Moody took it upon himself to confront employers and make a powerful plea on behalf of those who were being victimised. Soon, other middle-class black people in Britain joined him in his crusade for equal rights, and before long, they realised they would be more effective if they formed an organisation.

In 1931, the LCP was born, with Dr Moody serving as its founder and president. It became the first effective pressure group in Britain to work on behalf of its black citizens. Black people who had made Britain their home supported Dr Moody and the LCP, and they included Dr Cecil Belfield Clarke of Barbados, George A. Roberts of Trinidad, Samson Morris of Grenada, Robert Adams of British Guiana and Desmond Buckle of Ghana.

Dr Moody saw the organisation primarily as serving a Christian purpose, not a political one. Yet for two decades the LCP was the most influential organisation campaigning for the civil rights of African and Caribbean people in Britain. Through various campaigns and *The Keys*, a quarterly journal first published in 1933, the LCP struck many blows against racism in Britain. In 1939 the publication of *The Keys* was suspended because of lack of funds. During the war its place was taken by the monthly *News Letter*.

In 1941, in the *News Letter*, W. Arthur Lewis, a St Lucian and member of the LCP's executive committee, said:

> At the outbreak of this war spokesmen of the British Government made speeches denouncing the vicious racial policies of Nazi Germany and affirming that the British Empire stands for racial equality. It therefore seemed to the League ... that the time had come once more to direct the Government's attention to its own racial policy, and if possible to get these fine speeches crystallised into action.[2]

The height of the LCP's influence as a pressure group came in 1943 when the organisation held its twelfth Annual General Meeting in Liverpool. It was attended by over 500 people and one of the talks concerned 'a charter for colonial freedom'. The following year, the LCP drafted 'A Charter for Coloured People' and the text included a demand for self-government for all colonial peoples. It also declared that all racial discrimination in employment, restaurants, hotels and other public places should be made illegal and 'the same economic, educational, legal and political rights shall be enjoyed by all persons, male and female, whatever their colour'.

The charter foreshadowed the resolutions of 1945 Pan-African Congress in Manchester. The LCP was the forerunner of such organisations as the Race Relations Board (1965–76) and the Commission for Racial Equality (1976–2007). During the Second World War, when thousands of black workers and military personnel came to Britain from colonies in Africa and the Caribbean to support the war effort, Dr Moody's workload increased but it also gave him and the LCP greater purpose and influence.

When the Jamaican nationalist leader Marcus Garvey died in London on 10 June 1940, Dr Moody wrote a moving tribute in the LCP's *News Letter*. He described Garvey as one of the greatest men the LCP had been associated with, 'No other man operating outside Africa has so far been able to unite our people in such large numbers for any object whatsoever.'[3]

At the height of the London Blitz, in addition to his work as a GP and campaigner, Dr Moody continued to produce the *News Letter*, and in an editorial he said, 'Our work, such as the preparation of this letter, has to be carried on to the hum of hostile planes and the boom of friendly guns.'[4]

As the war intensified, Dr Moody's influence continued to grow. Towards the end of 1940, Dr Moody accepted an invitation to visit Buckingham Palace. On 12 December 1940, Her Majesty the Queen received a fleet of thirty-five mobile canteens in the forecourt of Buckingham Palace. The mobile canteens had been purchased and provided by the colonies on behalf of Britain. Dr Moody's lifelong friend and biographer, David A. Vaughan, described this important occasion in *Negro Victory* (1950), 'During the ceremony Moody was presented to the Queen [who] made enquiries concerning the welfare of the people of his race and displayed a real interest in them.'[5] The LCP's *News Letter* said:

> The canteens will serve hot drinks and food to people in London and other cities who have been bombed out of their homes, or who, during the winter, have to spend long and anxious nights in shelters away from their homes.[6]

Dr Harold Moody's younger brother, Ronald, was enjoying success as a sculptor in continental Europe when war clouds were looming. In 1938 he settled in Paris and married Helene Coppel-Cowan, an English painter. In June 1940, two days before Paris fell to the Germans, the couple were forced to leave the city, abandoning his sculptures. Thankfully, they were retrieved after the war.

After their escape from Paris, Ronald and Helene set out on foot and joined hordes of refugees making their way south. His niece, Cynthia, takes up the story, 'After two hazardous, drama-ridden weeks, they reached Marseille on 2 July. For the next five weeks they stayed at a small hotel, whilst exploring every conceivable means of getting back to England: to no avail.'[7]

Then Ronald fell ill, but in February 1941 they made an attempt to cross the Pyrenees into Spain. The attempt failed due to Ronald's poor health. Three months later Helene, who had valid papers, reluctantly accepted repatriation to England and Ronald, no longer having valid papers, was forced to go into hiding in order to avoid internment. After three months on the run, he made his second attempt to escape but was captured and imprisoned. Fortunately, he was able to withstand interrogation and was released after a week, whereupon he made a third attempt to escape. This time he succeeded. After two weeks in a safe house in Barcelona, he was sent to Madrid and thence via Gibraltar to Liverpool where he arrived in October 1941.

In 1943, when Ronald was interviewed by Una Marson (see Chapter 13) for BBC Radio's *Calling the West Indies*, he described what happened when he and Helene escaped from Paris two days before the German invasion:

> For days we walked miles and miles, sleeping under hedges … my wife's feet were bleeding profusely. Still, we trudged on and eventually arrived at Toulouse. There we were fortunate enough to get a train to take us to Marseilles. We arrived, thinking we would stay a week, but it was fifteen months later that I finally got away.

Ronald told Una that, following Helene's repatriation, he began to live the life of a hunted criminal:

> … changing my abode, on an average, every fortnight. I met with very many unexpected kindnesses in the shape of rooms and attics, and became very, very expert at dodging the police. Eventually, after three attempts, with a great deal of luck, I got away.[8]

4

Conscientious Objector

In 1941 the LCP offered the post of travelling secretary to Basil Rodgers, a member of the organisation from its inception. Rodgers had been born in Devon to a Jamaican father and an English mother. By 1941 Rodgers was well-known on the concert platform for his tenor singing voice. He began singing on BBC Radio as early as 1926 and in the 1930s he had given concerts and recitals at the famous Wigmore Hall in London. In 1932, a favourable review in *The Times* newspaper described the 'beautiful quality' of Rodgers' singing.[1]

Not everyone agreed with taking part in the Second World War and some refused military service, or any kind of work that supported the war effort. They were known as conscientious objectors, individuals who claimed the right to refuse military service on the grounds of freedom of thought, conscience or religion. Some even went to prison for making such a stand. In October 1941, the LCP's *News Letter* profiled Rodgers, and acknowledged:

> He recently appeared before a tribunal in Bristol to answer as a conscientious objector to war. The learned judge stated

that he had no doubt whatsoever about the sincerity of his convictions and gave him exemption to do the important work of Travelling Secretary to the League or failing that to carry on with his own present occupation. Mr. Rodgers feels, to quote his own words: 'that it is not enough to win the soil of a country, you must win the love and loyalty of its people. In the peace that is bound to come this love can never be won unless we, the coloured peoples, are represented not as serfs, but as equal partners in a great Commonwealth to carry out the Christian duty of the uplift of man.'[2]

However, Rodgers declined the offer of the post of travelling secretary. In the *News Letter*, he explained his reasons:

It is with deep regret, owing to the events of war and the fact that war brings out the worst characteristics possible from the otherwise human race that I find it impossible to become an active paid member of any organisation, without indirectly becoming part of the war machine, and unless one can feel that he is at one with his colleagues, in every detail, such a job as defending the rights of coloured people would be out of the question.[3]

5

Evacuees

On 1 September 1939, anticipating massive air raids, the British Government began to evacuate schoolchildren and mothers with infants under 5 years old from threatened cities. Further waves of evacuation followed in 1940. The hallmarks of every small evacuee were a gas mask, in its cardboard box, and a luggage label giving the name of the child.

Though many books and documentaries have been written and produced about Britain's 3.5 million evacuees, information about black evacuees is hard to find. A rare example is Ben Wicks' book *No Time to Wave Goodbye* (1988), in which he acknowledged the existence of black evacuees, but only fleetingly. He described John Jasper as one of five children in his family who were evacuated from the major industrial city of Manchester to Darwen in Lancashire. In a brief extract from their interview, Jasper described for Wicks his evacuation experience as a story of rags to riches. The vicarage where they stayed was 'like Buckingham Palace' and the children were taken on holidays to places like Blackpool and Wales where they stayed in four-star hotels, 'We lived in a lovely house just outside Preston with a farm and we were given a pony and a donkey. There were very few black people in Darwen and none at all outside Preston.'[1]

Ben Wicks also mentioned a small but revealing anecdote about two 'tiny black children', evacuees who were ignored in a school yard until a 'kind couple decided to give them a home'. A schoolteacher quoted by Wicks said, 'Imagine the surprise to the neighbourhood when their well-dressed parents turned up in a week's time with a carload of food and presents for the foster parents.'[2]

The two tiny black children were not alone in being ignored by potential foster parents. In some cases the problems experienced by black evacuees were reported to the LCP, who did everything they could to help. In one of their early wartime newsletters, published in November 1939, one such case from Blackpool was reported:

Among the large party of children which came to our district were two little coloured boys. Nobody wanted them. House after house refused to have them. Finally a very poor old lady of seventy years volunteered to care for them. She gave them a good supper, bathed them and put them to bed. As she folded their clothes she discovered two letters addressed to the person who adopted them. Each letter contained a five pound note.[3]

In an article on the BBC's website entitled 'WW2: The People's War', Trevor Sawtell recalled the 'multi-coloured' family who were sent to his village in the Welsh countryside. He said that, of all the evacuees in Ebbw Vale, none attracted more attention than the family who were sent to them from London:

Most of the people in Ebbw Vale had never seen a black person in the flesh. They were therefore considered very strange, rarities which must be observed at every opportunity: they were stared at in the street. People sitting in their homes would, on seeing one of them pass by a window, rush to their doors to stare long and hard at him or her. For a short while after their arrival, we children used to wait outside their house in the hope of seeing a member of this most peculiar family. Many women considered the white mother a 'fallen woman' for having broken what was then the taboo of marrying a black man. The family must have been aware of our offensive reaction to them. It was, in a sense, a kind of racism based on hurtful curiosity and the ignorance that comes of living in a quiet backwater, where anything outside the norm is sensational. Once people got used to the family, they became part of our community. They did not return to London after the war, but remained in Ebbw Vale and the surrounding areas, where the children married and raised children of their own. The fact is a salve to my conscience and perhaps the conscience of others, too.[4]

Only one black evacuee has ever been interviewed for a television documentary. On 3 September 1969, on the thirtieth anniversary of the outbreak of the Second World War, the BBC screened *Where Were You On the Day War Broke Out?* Among those interviewed was Joan Lloyd-Evans who, at the age of 4, had been sent from Liverpool to the safety of mid-Wales. She was also featured in an article in the *Radio Times*.

The strategic importance of the docks in Canning Town and Custom House in the East End made it one of London's most vulnerable areas. To avoid the intensive bombing that was expected, in 1939 many children were evacuated from the area, including Joseph, Joan and Christopher Cozier. The Cozier family lived on Sandford Street in Canning Town. The head of the household, Joseph Snr, was born in British Guiana and he had run away to sea at the age of 14. He eventually settled in the growing black community of London's East End.

A number of black families lived in the area around the Royal Group of Docks, even before the First World War. These docks were the largest in the world, and the Port of London was the most famous in the British Empire. Many black families lived in the streets around the 'sailortown' area of Victoria Dock Road, which ran from west to east from Canning Town to Custom House. The number of African and Caribbean seamen who settled in the area increased during the First World War. Situated off Victoria Dock Road, Crown Street was known locally as 'Draughtboard Alley' because black and white families lived side by side.[5]

In 1920 Joseph Cozier married an Englishwoman, Florence Tindling, and they had eight children. Their eldest daughter, Anita, has recalled that, when she was growing up, there were very few black women in their community, 'so black seamen married white women and quite a lot of mixed marriages turned out all right because they were good to each other. Where we lived there was no feeling that mixed marriages were wrong.'[6] Their son Christopher has described their father as a communist and:

> ... very educated. He could speak three languages ... he always found work. He took menial jobs on the railways. Dad was respected in our community. Everyone called him 'Mr. Cozier'. All the old coloured men were respected and addressed as 'Mr'. White and black people respected each other. When I grew up in the 1930s, racial prejudice did not exist in our community.[7]

When the war started, Anita left school at the age of 14 and went to work in a sweet factory in Silvertown. At the same time, 8-year-old Christopher was evacuated with his sister Joan (aged 12) and brother Joseph (aged 10) to Great Bedwyn, near Marlborough in Wiltshire. Joseph takes up the story:

> It was an experience I would never liked to have missed. We went with the school, St Joachim's, a catholic school in Custom House. There was a crowd of us from the East End, but we were the only coloured children. We were given our gas masks and the whole school was taken on a coach to a railway station and then we went off to a village. It was quite an adventure because we'd never left home before.[8]

The Cozier children were taken to the village hall in Great Bedwyn where the vicar and some women from the community offered different children to villagers for fostering. Each child had his or her name called out and was told to stand on the stage. The villagers came and picked the children they wanted, but the Coziers were left out. They only picked the white children, except a little boy who had impetigo. As Joseph recalled:

Afterwards there was just Joan, Chris, myself and this boy with impetigo left in the village hall. I thought to myself, 'I won't let this bother me'. I was with my brother and sister anyway. At the end of the day the vicar took us to his vicarage, but he wasn't married, and didn't have a clue how to look after us. So, he asked one of our teachers to feed us. But she was a spinster and couldn't cook either. Instead she fed us garibaldi biscuits with milk and raisins for breakfast, dinner and tea! When the health visitor came, she told the vicar we must be given proper meals.

Luckily for the Cozier children, Mrs MacDonald, an Irish woman who had been evacuated to the same village with her two daughters, knew their family and took them under her wing. Joseph described her as a 'lovely woman' who mended their clothes and took them for walks in the countryside. Said Joseph:

We were together for about two years. I don't know what would have happened to us if Mrs MacDonald hadn't been there. We had the run of the vicarage, and access to orchards and forests. We even had a canal, something we'd never seen before. It was a very happy experience. We roamed all over the countryside. It was an adventure. There was always something new to find out every day. Mum and Dad visited us when they could, and Dad wrote us letters. Mum couldn't read or write. When we returned to London, we had great difficulties adjusting. We lived right on the docks. We could see the funnels of the ships at the top of our street.

6

The Call of the Sea

Able Seaman James Bailey was among the many black and mixed-race merchant seamen who made the ultimate sacrifice for their king and country. He was the Liverpool-born son of Marcus Bailey, a Barbadian who had served in the merchant navy in the First World War. At the age of 24, James was killed in action on 14 March 1941 while serving on the SS *Western Chief*. It was sunk by the Italian submarine *Emo* in the North Atlantic Ocean. His younger sister, Lilian (see Chapters 2 and 17), later recalled, 'My brother Jim had been reported missing, but I hoped against hope that he had been picked up as I knew he sailed in convoy. The survivors of the ship were picked up, but Jim was not amongst them.'[1] James is remembered with honour at the Tower Hill Memorial in London.

Merchant navy galley boy, 'Tommy' Douglas of the SS *Hawkinge* was born in Cardiff, the son of Amizah and Sarah Ann Douglas. Lying about his age, he went to sea at the age of 14. He was just 15 years old on 27 July 1941 when he was killed on his second trip. The *Hawkinge*, a British cargo ship, was torpedoed in the Battle of the Atlantic, and sunk en route from Glasgow to Lisbon. She was carrying a cargo of 2,806 tons of coal when she was torpedoed by a German submarine and sunk. Fifteen men were lost from a crew of thirty-one.

In 2002, the five surviving siblings of Tommy Douglas were presented with his three medals in Butetown, Cardiff. Tommy's sister Patti said she only found out about the presentation after attending a memorial service for drowned sailors. Elder brother Billy told the *Western Mail* (on 31 July 2002) that Butetown had lost a lot of its sons during the Battle of the Atlantic when British merchant ships were attacked by German U-boats, 'All those boys went – and they went without a quibble – to do their duty.' Tommy is remembered with honour on Panel 56 at the Tower Hill Memorial in London.

By the end of 1940, around 6,000 merchant seamen had been killed. In 1941 at least 7,000 more lost their lives and in 1942 about 8,000 perished. In total, more than 50,000 British merchant seamen died as a result of enemy action in the Second World War. Sid Graham, a merchant seaman, remembered, 'You was always on edge. You could never settle down. If you were sleeping you always got something on your mind – like torpedoes. But you knew what you had signed on for when you went on the ship.'[2]

Before the war, young Sid Graham dreamed of following in his father's footsteps and going to sea. At the age of 15, he fulfilled his ambition and became a galley boy on the *Nernta*, a ship sailing to South America. From the 1930s to the 1950s Sid worked as a stoker on cargo boats operating from London. During the war, Sid served on Atlantic and Arctic convoys. It was dangerous work for it was merchant seamen such as Sid who suffered the most from the German U-boat (submarine) attacks.

Sid was born in Tidal Basin in London's East End in 1920. He was the son of Sidney 'Siddy' Graham, a seaman from Barbados, and his English wife, an East Ender called Emma. In an interview with the local historian Howard Bloch in 1993, Sid remembered that racism – or the 'colour bar' as it was then known – was an issue in Britain when he was growing up, except in his own community. He said, 'Canning Town, Tidal Basin, and Custom House, they were cosmopolitan, everybody lived round here: Africans, West Indians, Japanese, Chinese. Everybody got on.'[3]

Early in 1942, Sid was crossing the Atlantic on a supply ship, the SS *Scottish Star*. He recalled:

> Of course we were the lowest of the low, the stokers. They used to lock us in when an attack began … You're working your nuts off down there with them fires all the time. You think to yourself, Jesus, I wonder if we're going to make it or not. All sorts of silly things run through your head. You look and say, What's the best way if you can escape? You're looking for the best way for yourself. Every man for himself.[4]

On 19 February 1942, Sid was in the bathroom when an Italian submarine, the RIN *Luigi Torelli*, torpedoed the *Scottish Star*. The ship was abandoned. Sid recalled:

> When we got torpedoed I went up in the air and hit my ribs on the washbasin … busted 'em … I got up on the companionway and that's when the submarine started to shell us. We wasn't going down quick enough for him. I was badly hit in the arm. I went in the lifeboat and we got away from the ship and the ship went down … Luckily enough we were not in the cold, but we didn't know where we were going.[5]

The shipwrecked crew had no idea where they were because their voyage was a 'special operation'. Sid survived for ten days in the lifeboat with twenty other crew members. On the lifeboat, drinking water was strictly rationed and sharks could be seen in the sea. Sid recalled:

> They used to come and float around … give you a look. And you'd make a noise and beat the sides of the boat with the oar

and they'd float away. They can't stand noise we was told, so that's what we done. Happily it worked.[6]

The lifeboat drifted 600 miles and the survivors were tossed around the Atlantic Ocean, suffering from severe cold and seasickness and existing on meagre rations which included a couple of dry biscuits. When the men were picked up by a fishing boat from Barbados, they realised they had drifted into the Caribbean.[7] The fishing boat took Sid and the other survivors to Barbados. After landing, the Seamen's Mission gave them clothes and the local newspaper, *Barbados Advocate*, reported the story on their front page (28 February 1942).

Sid and the other survivors were shocked when their pay was stopped:

> In those days as soon as you got torpedoed on them ships your money was stopped right away … Only thing they give us was our clothes … we couldn't walk about *naked*, could we. It's hard to think what you been through and they treat you like that.[8]

Sid had never visited Barbados before. His father had come from the island and had relatives there, though Sid had never met them. Eventually, Sid's Aunt Dorothy was located, and she took him in. However, being wartime there was no way of letting his family know he was safe, and six months passed before a ship arrived to take him back to Britain. There were tears of joy when Sid was reunited with his parents and five younger siblings, 'My mother, God rest her soul, had been going crazy when I was away,' he later said.[9]

While Sid was in Barbados, his family had lost their London home in an air raid. They were rehoused, but Sid didn't know anything about it:

> When I came home, I couldn't find them! So I went to the police station to make enquiries, and I'm walking along with

me suitcase, and my mother was scrubbing the step of the house opposite the police station. 'Siddy!' she shouted out to my Dad, 'Daddy! Sidney's here!' And they all came out to welcome me home. But afterwards the police thought I was a deserter and Mum done her nut. Then they came and took me to work on special operational jobs all through the rest of the war. I went to every invasion there was. I won all the medals, including the Burma Star, but I had to send ten shillings for every medal I won. I gave them all to my children.

7

The London Blitz

The first air raids of the London Blitz, otherwise known as Hitler's blitzkrieg ('lightning war'), began on 7 September 1940. They were mainly aimed at the Port of London in the East End. The raids caused severe damage, which the Germans hoped would create a division between those living there and the rest of London. From mid-September to mid-November, air raids took place every day and night, and 30,000 were killed.

In October 1940, London experienced its worst air raid so far, when 400 Germans bombed the capital for six hours, and in one night, 29–30 December 1940, bombers caused the greatest destruction in the City of London since the Great Fire of 1666. Miraculously, St Paul's Cathedral survived, though ten churches also designed by Sir Christopher Wren were destroyed.

The London Blitz continued until 10–11 May 1941. By the end of this period, over 43,000 civilians had been killed and more than 1 million houses were destroyed or damaged. Important munitions and shipbuilding areas were targeted. While the Germans never again managed to bomb London on such a large scale, they carried out smaller attacks throughout the war.

There had been occasional air raids on Britain in June, July and August 1940. It was during this period that the American-born singer Adelaide Hall found herself facing danger when she made an appearance in South London. Adelaide topped the bill of a variety show at the Lewisham Hippodrome with her piano accompanist, Gerry Moore.

On the evening of 26 August, in the middle of her act, the air-raid siren sounded, but most of the audience remained seated. When the raid started, everyone in the theatre could hear the screaming bombs falling and exploding, and the bursts of anti-aircraft machine-gun fire. Though the building was strongly constructed, the blasts of exploding bombs close by was clearly felt in the auditorium. Adelaide encouraged the nervous audience to join her in some community song numbers and she later recalled:

> We – the performers and the audience – were told that no one could leave the theatre because it was too dangerous. Outside everything was burning. So, we just carried on and I managed to get the audience to join in many of the songs.[1]

For four hours, with bombs exploding outside the Lewisham Hippodrome, Adelaide helped to entertain the nervous audience until the all clear sounded at 3.45 a.m. Though Adelaide could barely speak, in defiant mood she returned to the stage of the Hippodrome the following evening to perform her act as scheduled.

In the United States, Adelaide's bravery at the Lewisham Hippodrome made news. America hadn't entered the war yet and Adelaide was one of only a handful of American stars who had remained in Britain to entertain the public and the troops. Under various headlines, 'Adelaide Hall in Bombing, Calmly Singing Songs' and 'It Rained Bombs as Adelaide Sang', accounts of Adelaide's fighting spirit flashed across America and reached the front pages of many newspapers.

Adelaide continued her concert tour around Britain. She later reflected:

> When we performed during air raids, we learned to be philo-
> sophical about the dangers we were being exposed to. Of
> course, in situations like the one at Lewisham Hippodrome are
> a little different, but we carried on to keep the public's morale
> from becoming too low.[2]

When the London Blitz began, not all children had been evacuated. Some stayed with their families because they were considered too young, or because their parents preferred to keep them close by. Kenny Lynch was born in the East End, one of the Germans' main targets, and lived with his family in Cornwall Street, Stepney. Kenny was the youngest of thirteen children born to a Barbadian father, Oscar Lynch, a merchant seaman, and an English mother, Amelia. Kenny recalled that he was too young to join his brothers and sisters, who were evacuated to north Wales:

> I stayed behind with my mum and dad because you had
> to be older to be evacuated. I just remember it being a
> very funny time. We used to go down these air-raid shel-
> ters every night, and we were bombed out of about three
> houses. We just used to move in with the person next door,
> or into one of the houses that was still standing. We must
> have moved about four or five times. I remember it as if
> it happened only yesterday. I can remember watching our
> house get bombed as the sirens went. We walked out of the
> house, got about four or five hundred yards away, and this
> great big flame went up. My old man said to me, 'That's
> our house. So, we'll probably move in with somebody else
> tomorrow'. And then we'd go down the shelter and every-
> body would be singing. As a kid growing up, I remember it
> as a great fun time.[3]

In Fulham, Joseph Bruce stayed at home when the London Blitz started. His daughter Esther said he took a chance – 'a lot of people did' – but she played safe and went to the public shelter with her neighbours. She recalled:

One night we all had to get out of there. The Germans surrounded it with incendiary bombs. They were fire bombs which the Germans were dropping so that the others who followed could find Earl's Court, which was very close to where we lived. One little lad said he could hear something ticking and his mum told him to shut up. Then the air-raid warden came in and told us we had to get out. A bomb had landed right behind the shelter and didn't explode. I had an old girl sitting near me. That was poor old Mrs Clark. She said: 'Will you take me to the shelter at the other end of the street, Esther?' I said: 'Of course I will, love.' But it was quite a long way to the other shelter and the Germans were going hell for leather. Bombs were falling everywhere and there was broken glass on the ground. Mrs Clark was hanging onto me. We got out of the shelter in Eli Street and went with the neighbours through the air raid and into the one in Hilmer Street. It was packed. As for being scared, I just didn't think about it.[4]

Esther recalled the friendliness and community spirit that existed during the Blitz:

You'd be walking along and the air-raid siren would go, and people opened their doors and shouted: 'Come in here, love' and they would give you shelter. People are not like that today. During the war people were very friendly. I think the war, in a way, made people more friendly but after the war people changed.

As Esther Bruce testified, the London Blitz brought people together. Her overriding memory of the Blitz was of friendliness and community spirit. However, the same could not be said for a housewife who was the same age as Esther, also mixed race, and living in another part of London. In 1941 the prime minister, Winston Churchill, received a letter from the housewife, who was living in poor accommodation in Camden Town in North London. She described herself as the daughter of an Englishwoman and a West Indian father and married to a West African who was employed on demolition work. In her letter, the housewife pleaded with the prime minister to address the discrimination faced by some black citizens in wartime. 'Can't something be done,' she asked. 'After all, we are British subjects. If this letter is received by you I hope it will not be cast aside.'[5]

The letter was not cast aside but forwarded to the Social Services Department of Downing Street. In a reply to the housewife, it was suggested that she make an appointment with John L. Keith, a Welfare Officer in the Colonial Office, to discuss with him the issues she raised. During the war years, Keith investigated the problems faced by many members of Britain's black community. He maintained a liberal approach to the situations he encountered.

Following the meeting between the housewife and Keith, he drafted a report on 29 October 1941 in which he described her as 'an intelligent and sensible woman', who told him about 'the difficulties which working-class coloured people have in finding decent and reasonably priced accommodation in London'. She also explained the difficulties faced by black people in Camden Town, who were badly treated by air-raid wardens and police officers, who ejected them from air-raid shelters and the underground 'as if they were Jews in Germany'.[6] Keith advised the housewife to encourage black people who had been subjected to acts of racism to come and see him at the Colonial Office, and he assured her that he would discuss her complaints with the Chief Warden of the Camden Town ARP and a senior police officer.

★★★

The civilians of London had an important role to play in the protection of their city. The main objective of Germany's leader, Adolf Hitler, was to destroy the morale of the civilian population, but he failed. Many civilians who were not willing or able to join the military became members of the Home Guard, the ARP service, the Auxiliary Fire Service (AFS), and many other organisations.

E.I. Ekpenyon, a Nigerian from the town of Calabar who came to Britain to study law, began training as a warden with the ARP service as soon as the war broke out. As an air-raid warden in St Marylebone, Ekpenyon worked as an official in charge of local arrangements for air raids. He was responsible for running air-raid shelters, giving advice to his community, keeping lists of people living locally, helping with rescue work and warning people about the blackout. (During the war, all outside lights were switched off and people had to make sure that no lights could be seen from within their homes – hence people put up 'blackout' screens or curtains.)

According to his daughter, Oku Ekpenyon, her father carried out his ARP duties conscientiously and she described one event, during a night raid in the London Blitz, which always remained in his mind. Her father was standing on the top of a 100ft-high building when he saw the sky light up with searchlights and heard the shells of anti-aircraft guns bursting as fires started in different parts of the city. Oku explained that, as a senior warden, her father regularly went out on patrols to ensure that the blackout was enforced. He also kept a 'census' of people in private and business premises – essential information when a building was bombed. She said:

> He had a day and night off work each week but that did not stop people in his sector turning up on his doorstep if they needed him. My father's popularity locally showed the ambivalence that existed when he had problems with one of his shelters. The shelterers were of many different nationalities and beliefs. The bombing had forced them into one another's

company, a situation that would never have happened in normal times.[7]

In a pamphlet published in 1943, entitled *Some Experiences of an African Air Raid Warden*, Ekpenyon described how he challenged racism in the air-raid shelters:

Some of the shelterers told others to go back to their own countries, and some tried to practice segregation. So I told the people that though I am an air-raid warden in London I am still an African. I said I would like to see a spirit of friendliness, co-operation and comradeship prevail at this very trying time in the history of the Empire. I further warned my audience that if what I had said was not going to be practised, I would advise those who did not agree to seek shelter somewhere else.[8]

He added:

It amuses me to know that in the district where I work the people believe that because I am a man of colour I am a lucky omen. I had heard of such childish beliefs, but I am delighted that such beliefs exist, for wherever my duties take me the people listen to my instructions and orders, and are willing to allow me to lead them. So I am able to control them, which makes my duties lighter in these troublous days.[9]

During the war, Ekpenyon made several broadcasts for BBC Radio's Empire Service in *Calling West Africa*. In the first broadcast he made, on 11 July 1941, he described his duties as an air-raid warden, such as tackling the fires started by incendiary bombs, and he recalled several frightening experiences during air raids. On one occasion, he had to evacuate a shelter that had suffered bomb damage. In his pamphlet, Ekpenyon elaborated on his experiences of this particular incident:

I found the shelter had been damaged and was in darkness, and about 120 people were in a state of confusion. As I was standing on the top of the stairs, I shone my torch on my face and signalled to them to be quiet. I managed to make myself heard, and told them plainly that if they wanted to be saved from fire they had to keep cool and take orders from me. Failing that, they and I would have to remain in the building and face our fate, which would be a very unpleasant one. The people became quiet and we were able to evacuate everyone…
I had to carry a frightened woman from the damaged shelter. In the street the droning of the planes and the bursting shells increased her fright, so that she gripped me round the neck and I was nearly choked. I braced myself and carried her to a place of safety.[10]

The LCP's wartime newsletters are an invaluable source of information about black civilian defence workers. After the Blitz started, the LCP began to publish reports about the contribution made by black citizens. For instance, in December 1940, A.A. Thompson, the Jamaican academic and General Secretary of the LCP, praised the work of black 'front liners'. He said:

In London especially one is amazed at the numbers of coloured men who have accommodated themselves to the novel circumstances of the war, and are to be found working as wardens, AFS [Auxiliary Fire Service] men, members of stretcher parties, first aid units, and mobile canteens. One feels that the contribution these men are making to the defence of London ought to be given the fullest publicity.[11]

Thompson named some of the black 'front liners' he encountered, though he was careful not to break wartime censorship and identify where they were located. For example, he described Mr Headley, a mining engineer from British Guiana, as 'the respected warden of an area that has repeatedly been bombed'.

In his report, Thompson concluded, 'the contribution of the coloured population in proportion to its numbers is pretty considerable. This fact should be acknowledged.'

George A. Roberts, who was also mentioned in Thompson's report, lived in Warner Road, Camberwell, in south-east London. As a brave fire fighter, he faced constant danger throughout the London Blitz. He put out fires and saved lives while the bombs fell and exploded. George was a Trinidadian who had served in the First World War in the Middlesex Regiment. It is likely that George's First World War experience on the battlefields of Loos, the Somme and in the Dardanelles prepared him for this onslaught.

When the Second World War began, George was too old for combat, so he trained with the AFS, which was known as the National Fire Service (NFS) from 1941. His base was New Cross Fire Station and in 1943 he was made a section leader. George was also responsible for organising the Discussion and Education Groups of the wartime NFS. He realised that fire officers had time on their hands between air raids and the discussion groups helped them to relieve the boredom and tension. As such, George met and befriended a number of prominent artists and writers, including Norman Hepple, who painted his portrait. In 1944, George was awarded the British Empire Medal which was presented to him by King George VI at Buckingham Palace.

When war was declared, Fernando Henriques was a Jamaican-born resident of London whose immediate reaction was to join the armed forces:

> There was no thought that through my colour I would be thought to be outside the conflict. My experience at the recruiting centre in central London was traumatic. An RAF sergeant told me quite bluntly that 'wogs', that is people of non-European descent, were not considered officer material. That of course was in 1939. A year later, as Britain became pressed, the situation became quite different. I cannot say that

disgust invaded me totally at this rejection. It was rather like being confronted with hatred by someone you loved and thought loved you.[12]

Rejected by the RAF, Fernando decided to defend London in another capacity. He joined the AFS in September 1939 and remained a fireman for three years:

Told on the outbreak of war that I was not white enough to fly, I was permitted to defend London in another capacity. With a friend from schooldays – inevitably white – I joined the Auxiliary Fire Service. We were accepted with enthusiasm, for in those days it was thought London would be inundated with fire bombs almost immediately. Issued with uniforms, we were swiftly assigned to one of the improvised fire stations which had mushroomed all over the city on the outbreak of war.[13]

The 'improvised fire station' referred to by Fernando was a requisitioned middle-class girls' school in Maresfield Gardens in Hampstead. At the Maresfield Gardens AFS, Fernando befriended the poet Stephen Spender, novelist William Sansom and the artist Leonard Rosoman, who began making paintings of his experiences as a fire-fighter during the London Blitz. Fernando described the fire service in London in those days as a kind of refuge for intellectuals. He said:

Many of the long-haired brigade had joined the armed forces but many also opted for civil defence, which was a reserved occupation. All classes were represented in these services and, because of the atmosphere induced by the common crisis of war, fire stations and the like became a kind of utopian democracy. In my own case, located in an inner suburb of London's Hampstead – which has always had a reputation for liberalism and creativity – firemen were everything from greengrocers to poets … The working-class element in the station respected

the intellectual group which by a process of osmosis both educated, and were educated.[14]

As a fireman during air raids, Fernando found himself con-
stantly on the alert, but 'the Fire Service provided long
periods of standing-by when I could study. This I did, and to
the surprise of both my friends and myself obtained an Open
Scholarship to Oxford.'[15]

In the June 1941 edition of the LCP's *News Letter*, Fernando
highlighted the discrimination faced by some black men when
they attempted to join the ARP. He described the experience
of a friend who put his name down at the local town hall for
enrolment as a full-time warden, only to be rejected when
he attended the opening lecture for the warden's course. He
demanded to see someone in authority, but when he came face
to face with the controller of the department, he was told that
there was no room for black people in the ARP. Aggrey House,
a centre for colonial students set up by the government in
Bloomsbury, central London, took up the case, and Fernando's
friend received an apology from the controller. Said Fernando,
'He is very happy in his job and has won the respect of both
officers and men in his depot.'

In the same article, Fernando listed the names of the some
of the black ARP workers in the London area, and noted that
St Pancras 'has a particularly strong coloured ARP section',
including the following stretcher bearers who all possessed
the certificate of the St John's Ambulance Brigade: Chick
Alexander and Sam Blake (Jamaica), Charles Allen and A.K.
Lewis (Freetown, Sierra Leone), Laryea (Accra), Ote Johnson
and A. Kester (Nigeria) and E. Gonzaley (Trinidad). He added
that D.E. Headley (British Guiana) was the head warden at
St Pancras, G.A. Roberts (Trinidad) was a leading auxiliary in
the AFS at the New Cross Fire Station, and Billy Williams from
Sierra Leone was a warden at St Marylebone. 'But the list is
endless,' he added.

Every London borough has at least one representative of the coloured population in London ... Coloured people as a whole have really come forward and shown their willingness to co-operate with the people of Britain in their titanic struggle. Despite all setbacks we are fighting in the front line, and will continue to do so. We are more than proud to say that the coloured population of London and Britain have come forward in this way.[16]

In spite of the London Blitz, Adelaide Hall continued to entertain the British public. An engagement to sing at an anti-aircraft site in Regent's Park was particularly frightening:

The first time I played there an air raid started and, when the guns started blasting, I thought my head was going to be blown off when they opened up! I'd never heard such a loud bang-bang. I turned to my pianist and asked: 'Are you all right, Ron?' He looked terrified and said, very quietly: 'Just about.' I was singing at another anti-aircraft site in Green Park when we heard the air-raid siren. They told me to keep on singing but to stop when I saw the red light. Then I had to run to the shelter. It was very scary.[17]

In October 1940, during a period of intensive bombing, Adelaide had a premonition that the popular New Florida nightclub, which she owned with her husband, Bert, was going to be hit. She told everyone to leave the club before the air raid started. Bert ignored his wife. He told her that if a bomb had his name on it, it would find him. He stayed, but Adelaide took flight, and left London with her secretary.

When the air-raid siren warned of an impending raid, Bert took refuge in the cellar with the club's barman. As the raid intensified, Bert and the barman became increasingly intoxicated. Afterwards, he told Adelaide that he couldn't remember anything about the club being hit. Bert and the barman were saved because they had sheltered in the cellar.

An entry in Adelaide's diary for 14 October confirmed the incident. The bombing of the New Florida was also included in the ARP warden's log which gave the time of the incident as 9.30 p.m. The type of bomb was described as a high explosive, and the total number of casualties was ten.[18]

After being conscripted for war work, Esther Bruce took a job as a cleaner in Brompton Hospital. She said:

I cleaned three wards. One was called the forces ward. This is where they put boys who had been wounded serving with the army, navy and air force. I had a smashing time in there. The pranks those boys got up to! I had to clean the ward the old-fashioned way. Down on my hands and knees with the polish and the buffer. I had a lot of fun in the forces ward. When the boys knew I was coming back on duty for the evening shift they asked me to bring them fish and chips. I had to smuggle this in otherwise matron would have had a fit![19]

Esther also learned to overcome her fear of air raids with the help of a young child:

When the air-raid siren started, I was told I could leave the ward I was cleaning and take shelter in the basement. But some patients couldn't be moved. Staff had to carry on as though nothing was happening because they didn't want to upset the patients. I was polishing the children's ward when an air raid started. I was talking to a little girl called Fiona at the time but I couldn't bring myself to leave. She couldn't have been more than three. I shall never forget that little kid. She was recovering from a serious operation. I'd always been frightened of air raids. After Fiona and I heard the siren we could hear bombs falling and exploding. Then the anti-aircraft guns started blasting. I was scared stiff but I couldn't leave Fiona. I held her hand but she could see I was shaking and asked, 'Are you frightened of air raids?' I didn't want to disturb her so I said, 'No, love. I'm not frightened.' She said: 'Don't be frightened. I'm here. They won't hurt you.' Afterwards I thought, well, if a little kid's not frightened, what the hell have I got to be scared of? That child taught me how to live through air raids.[20]

In addition to cleaning wards, Esther volunteered to work as a fire guard or fire watcher at the hospital. This position came about as a result of the night of Sunday, 29 December 1940, when the City of London was devastated by incendiary bombs. These were dropped in clusters to spread fires and to light the way for the high-explosive bombers. When the fire watchers scheme began in January 1941 it was made compulsory to have a person or persons on guard in buildings for twenty-four hours (in 'prescribed areas') to put out incendiary bombs and call for help. This proved difficult for many establishments to staff, and this led the government to implement a compulsory scheme of fire watching.

On 15 February 1941, Esther's father Joseph was knocked down by a taxi in the blackout. The incident, which happened in Abingdon Street, Westminster, just by the Palace of Westminster, led to his death at the age of 60. On the previous evening he had been returning home from work and took shelter when an air raid started. He remained in the shelter until morning when the all-clear sounded. Said Joshua Levine in *The Secret History of the Blitz*, 'Esther's father was one of 9,169 people killed in traffic accidents in 1941 – the highest figure ever recorded for a single year.'[21]

Esther was left on her own, but not for long. She was 'adopted' by one of her neighbours, 63-year-old Hannah Johnson, fondly known as 'Granny'. Esther came to look upon her as the mother she never had. Hannah's granddaughter, Kathy, said:

They had a sense of fun and knew how to enjoy themselves. Gran and Esther got on well together, and they were together for a long time. Gran was like a mother to Esther. As far as I can remember Esther was the only black person living in our area. She was part of our community. People knew her. She made friends with everyone. She was always chatting to someone in the street.[22]

Esther recalled how Granny took care of her, and how the air raids brought their community together, especially in their local air-raid shelter:

> When I came home from work and went to the air-raid shelter I found Granny cooking our tea. They had fires in there, and stoves, and we'd stay in there the whole evening and all through the night. We had a good time in the shelter. It was warm. We had sing-songs and bunks to sleep on. When a neighbour came in we welcomed them. Everybody was equal and pulled together. If somebody came into the shelter who we didn't know we said: 'Hello, love. Where do you come from?' We didn't turn anybody away. Sometimes during air-raids the bombs came a bit *too* close and it got scary, but I don't think the shelter would have stopped a bomb from killing us if one had hit it.[23]

During the war, food was rationed and, when the situation worsened, whale meat went on sale. Esther commented, 'I wouldn't eat it. I didn't like the look of it. We made a joke about it, singing Vera Lynn's song with new words: "Whale meat again!"'

Esther was lucky to have relatives in British Guiana. Now and again, she would turn to them for help and ask if they could send food parcels. 'They had an American base nearby, so they were better off than us,' she said:

> I asked Granny: "What grub do we need?" and wrote a letter. Two weeks later a bloody great big box arrived with tins of food. They helped us all through the war. We welcomed those food parcels.[24]

On 8 March 1941, the same day that Joseph Bruce died from the injuries he sustained, another Guyanese settler was killed in

London. His name was Ken 'Snakehips' Johnson, and he was the frontman for the popular West Indian Dance Orchestra.

Ken was arguably one of the most famous black men in Britain at that time, projecting an image of a gentleman about town: handsome, elegant and well over 6ft tall. With his extra-long baton, he led the smart white-jacketed orchestra, providing a class act. At the Café de Paris, the band became the toast of London's West End. When the café was 'wired' for BBC Radio broadcasts, the band's frequent appearances on the air waves helped to raise their profile with the British public. They successfully broke through to the mainstream of British entertainment with their radio broadcasts and appearances on the variety stage.

Ken's main achievement was to show that Britain could produce a black bandleader as sensational and classy as African Americans like Cab Calloway and Duke Ellington. Everyone who met Ken commented on how kind and gentle he was. He always found something nice to say about everyone. Outside of music, he loved good food, wines and, above all, a cigar. Sailing was one of his favourite pastimes.

Offstage, Ken was the lover of Gerald Hamilton, a memoirist and critic who was older than Ken and had led a somewhat controversial life. Hamilton had served prison sentences for bankruptcy, theft, gross indecency and even for being a threat to national security. He had calmed down by the time he met Ken in 1940. They made a home for themselves in Kinnerton Street, Belgravia.

During the London Blitz, the couple acquired a Thameside cottage called 'Little Basing' in Bray in Berkshire, where Ken indulged his passion for sailing. After appearing at the café, Ken would drive to the cottage, arriving in the early hours of the morning, but still have the energy to be up and about in the morning and out sailing on the River Thames until late afternoon, until it was time to return to London's West End and the club. These were happy times for Ken and Gerald.

In the first year of the war, Ken reached the peak of his popularity and the Café de Paris, situated underground, directly beneath the Rialto Cinema on Coventry Street, was thought to be impregnable. It was advertised by its owner, Martin Poulsen, as 'the safest and gayest restaurant in town – even in air raids. Twenty feet below ground.' Poulsen deluded the public into thinking there were four solid storeys of masonry above. Said Charles Graves in his history of the Café de Paris, 'All that protected the Café from a direct hit were the glass roof of the Rialto Cinema and the ceiling of the Café de Paris itself.'[25]

At 9.30 p.m. on Saturday, 8 March 1941, Ken was having drinks with some friends at the Embassy Club before his show at the Café, which was not far away. It was one of the worst nights of the Blitz and an air raid was raging. No taxi was available. His friends begged him to stay, but Ken was determined to arrive on time for his appearance.

Throughout the blackout and the falling bombs, Ken ran all the way from the Embassy Club to the Café de Paris. He was determined not to miss his show. He arrived at 9.45 p.m. and took his place on the bandstand. Five minutes later, two high-explosive bombs crashed onto the dance floor. One exploded in front of the bandstand. Charles Graves described the devastation, 'There was a flash like the fusing of a gigantic electric cable. All the lights went out. Masonry and lumps of plaster could be heard crashing to the ground.'[26]

Band member Joe Deniz was there. He later recalled that the band had just started playing their signature tune 'Oh Johnny', when the glass ceiling of the club was shattered:

As we started to play there was an awful thud, and all the lights went out. The ceiling fell in and the plaster came pouring down. People were yelling. A stick of bombs went right across Leicester Square, through the Café de Paris, and further up to Dean Street. The next thing I remember was being in a small van which had been converted into an ambulance. Then someone came to me and said: 'Joe, Ken's dead.' It broke me up.[27]

Reports of the numbers of dead and injured vary, but most agree that over thirty people lost their lives that night at the Café de Paris, including its owner. Sixty others were seriously injured.

One casualty was the Trinidadian saxophonist Dave 'Baba' Williams. He had been cut in half by the blast. Ken, however, was discovered without a mark on his body, his red carnation still in the buttonhole of his tailcoat. According to Philip Ziegler in *London at War 1939–1945*, in the aftermath looters:

> ... prowled around the floor of the shattered nightclub, ripping open handbags, tearing rings off the hands of the dead and the unconscious. There was an epidemic of looting during the blitz, so serious that Scotland Yard set up a special squad to deal with it.[28]

The actor Ballard Berkeley, later known for his role as Major Gowen in the sitcom *Fawlty Towers*, was working in his spare time as a special constable. He was one of the first to arrive on the scene:

> The explosion within this confined space was tremendous. It blew legs off people, heads off people, and it exploded their lungs so that when I went into this place, I saw people sitting at tables quite naturally. Dead. Dressed beautifully without a mark on them. Dead. It was like looking at waxworks.[29]

In *The People's War*, Angus Calder described the macabre scenes as 'among the most indelibly horrifying of the period'.[30]

Coverage of the incident in newspapers was delayed because there existed in wartime Britain strict government restrictions on the reporting of air-raid casualties. Newspapers were expected to maintain a balance between news and keeping up the morale of the public. At first, the incident at the Café de Paris was played down and it took time for the facts, including the tragic death of Ken, to be made known. Some early press reports gave a clue to the location in London in the song title, 'Oh Johnny'. Many associated this song with Ken and his orchestra. It was their 'theme' song. If readers knew this, they could probably work out which nightclub had been hit.

Ken was survived by his mother in British Guiana. Following his funeral, she gave consent for his ashes to remain in Britain. Arrangements for Ken's final resting place were made by Ken's friend, Ivor Cummings (see Introduction and Chapter 10), who contacted the headmaster of Ken's former school, Sir William Borlase's, and requested permission for the ashes to be interred in the school's chapel. On 8 March 1942, one year after he was killed, Ken's ashes were interred during a memorial service at the chapel.

Britain's first black swing band was no more, and its surviving members went their separate ways. While he was alive, Ken Johnson's fame only lasted a few years, but he made a big impact on the British public, who mourned his tragic death. The fact that the nickname 'Snakehips' is still referenced in popular television programmes such as *Strictly Come Dancing* is a testament to his legendary status in British showbusiness.

As for his partner, Gerald Hamilton, he was devastated. Thereafter, Gerald never travelled anywhere without the framed photograph of the young man he called 'My Husband'.[31]

★★★

In spite of the intensive bombing of Elephant and Castle and the surrounding area, the Barbadian Dr Cecil Belfield Clarke continued to work at his practice. It was located at 112 Newington Causeway and Clarke worked there all through the Blitz. He had been practising as a family GP at the address since 1920 and, away from his surgery, he became a founder member of the LCP. Dr Clarke's home was in New Barnet, and he named it 'Belfield House'. He shared this with his partner, Edward 'Pat' Walter, who was entered in the 1939 Register of England and

Wales as Dr Clarke's surgery assistant, secretary and housekeeper. Before the decriminalisation of homosexuality in 1967, many gay couples who wanted to live together managed to avoid detection by pretending that one of them, usually a professional, employed the other.

The worst air raid to hit Elephant and Castle took place on 10–11 May 1941, when German bombers targeted the area to create a terrible fire storm. Much of Elephant and Castle lay in ruins, a shadow of its pre-war days. Miraculously, Dr Clarke's surgery survived, as he explained in a letter to Una Marson (see Chapter 13) at the BBC. It is dated 10 June 1941.

Una had wanted Dr Clarke to make a broadcast about the Blitz in her series *Calling the West Indies*, but the bombing had caused him great distress. He asked Marson if he could postpone the broadcast for at least four weeks. He informed her that everything had gone in Newington Causeway, except his surgery. One complete side of the building was missing with all the rooms open to the elements. In spite of tarpaulins on the roof, rain was getting in, and he was writing the letter in his hat and coat. His gas and water supplies had been disconnected. In spite of this, Dr Clarke never closed his surgery.

***

When Earl Cameron (see Chapter 1), a young merchant seaman, came back to London in 1941, he faced the horrors of the Blitz:

Arriving at Euston station, I had a rather good feeling; it was like coming back home. I went back to Whitfield Street. The landlady at No. 63 said she was full, but another Italian landlady at No. 61 could put me up. I soon got a job at the Savoy Hotel as a kitchen porter. I had been working there for a few months, keeping, so to speak, the wolf from the door and experiencing many air raids on London. I soon resigned myself to the fact that if my number was up, so be it. I, like many others in London in those days, became very philosophical about the war and the bombings. There was no choice. The war was on, London was one of the main targets, and truly there was nowhere to hide. To go down and sleep in one of the many subway train stations as many people did was not, in any way, appealing to me. In any case, most of the time, the raids would take place around the shipping docks and the industrialised areas.[32]

On 10–11 May 1941, when London was targeted in another heavy air raid, the House of Commons was hit. In total, 1,212 people were killed in the capital that night. Londoners like Earl were unprepared for the ferociousness of this particular raid:

As I had to get up early in the morning, I would go to bed around 10 o'clock at night. I was in bed reading the evening newspaper when I heard the big guns going in the distance and within a couple of minutes, the alarm went. It was always a bad sign when you heard the guns before the alarm. Soon, I heard the sound of planes and the bombing, and the explosion of buildings. Then, the sound of a dive bomber with its diesel engine which one could not mistake because of its humming sound.

Earl said the first bomb he heard had the frightening whistling sound and then there was an explosion somewhere in the distance:

Then came the second bomb with a much louder whistling sound and the tremendous explosion that shook the whole area and then the third one with the whistling. I got out of bed and knelt down crying out to God, 'Please, please, help me'. The whistling sound got louder and I truly thought this is it and then the whistling got fainter and somewhere in the distance an explosion that merely shook the area. I quickly put on my trousers and made my way to the underground station in Goodge Street which was merely a matter of five minutes away. Practically the whole of Tottenham Court Road was alight. Maples furniture store was on fire. On the corner of Goodge Street and Tottenham Court Road was a shoe shop. I had been admiring some of the shoes there and now they were strewn all across the pavement and the glass from the front window was broken. The whole of London looked like a very big Guy Fawkes night. The wardens at the tube station were telling people to get down below. The station was packed with people. After about an hour or two, it became very claustrophobic and the heat was uncomfortable. I decided to have a look back up on the street and see what was going on, hoping that the bombing had stopped. It was quiet so I decided to go to the corner of Tottenham Court Road and Oxford Street where there was a Lyons Corner House and have a cup of hot chocolate.

There were four Lyons Corner Houses in London at that time: Oxford Street, the Strand, one near Piccadilly Circus and one in Marble Arch. They opened all night and were very popular but, during a quiet period, Earl decided to make his way to his favourite Lyons in Oxford Street. An air-raid warden told him he was crazy to go out because the German planes were coming in relays. The warden knew they would be back for sure. Earl said: 'I'll take my chance':

The walk to the corner of Oxford Street was about 8 to 10 minutes. Everything was still quiet, only a few guns in the distance, perhaps coming from the East End of London. After having a nice hot chocolate, I decided to make my way back to Goodge Street Station. Half way down Tottenham Court Road, the guns started to go and the Luftwaffe was back. There were explosives everywhere. The bombs were dropping overhead. I could hear that terrible sound of the heavy diesel bombers. I began to run. I felt like the size of an ant with all the noise over my head, the sound of the big guns and the noise of the dive bombers and shrapnel hitting the street. I kept running until I reached Goodge Street Station. The air-raid warden had said it would be foolish to go out as the bombers would be coming back again. I was very lucky that I was not hit by shrapnel as many people got killed from it. I went back down below and stayed there until daybreak when we got the all clear.

The next morning, on his way to work, Earl saw a London that had been torn apart. He said there was a look of despair on the faces of people. But life still went on. Buses ran, trains for the most part left on time and Winston Churchill was still alive and kicking. Although part of Buckingham Palace was hit, the royal family were still very much intact:

As hard as they tried, the Luftwaffe were unable to keep up this kind of air attack. They were trying to break the morale of the British people, but the people of this country were far too resilient. Soon after these big raids on the West End of London, the Germans invaded Russia. Life became somewhat more tolerable. The air-raids continued from time to time, but not nearly as drastic as on 10 May 1941.

8

Liverpool, Cardiff, Manchester and Plymouth

Liverpool, especially the docklands area, was the most heavily bombed city outside London. The first major air raid on Liverpool took place on 28 August 1940 when 160 German bombers attacked. On 28 November, a heavy raid on the city was described by Prime Minister Winston Churchill as the 'single worst incident of the war', when a direct hit on an air-raid shelter caused 166 fatalities.

In Liverpool's culturally diverse community, Grace Wilkie, the daughter of an African seaman and an English mother, lived with her husband. She was expecting a baby when the Blitz was at its worst. In 1991, when Grace was interviewed in the BBC Television series *Black Britain*, she described going into labour during an air raid on Liverpool on 10 January 1941:

There was bombs dropping all over the place, anti-aircraft guns going. It was terrible. And we had to have torchlight to bring my son Derry into the world because that night they dropped a bomb right behind where we lived. The hole in the ground was immense. It took away half the street. A lot of houses went that night. Some people got gassed on their premises and through all this I was giving birth to Derry. There was nothing I could do. There was no where I could go. It was a bad, bad raid.[1]

Butetown, in the Welsh capital of Cardiff, was an example of a culturally diverse community pulling together for the war effort. Though not as badly hit by bombing as Swansea, Plymouth, London and Coventry, parts of Cardiff – including Butetown – sustained heavy bombing because of the docks and munitions factories. In the February 1942 issue of the LCP's *News Letter* there was acknowledgement of the work of Cardiff's 'coloured front liners':

> They have stood up to enemy action with courage and calmness. Many of the women are helpers at the Rest Centre and during a 'blitz' in January last, helped to entertain and feed over three hundred and sixty people evacuated from their homes.[2]

In his book, *Negroes in Britain* (1948), Kenneth Little acknowledged that in some air-raid wardens' posts, 'on a minor scale, and with some different nationalities involved, an interesting illustration of international and inter-racial co-operation is afforded'.[3] Little was referring to the two air-raid wardens' posts in Cardiff: one at the Anglican church and the other at the Wesleyan Methodist church at the other end of the district. The latter's staff included a Maltese boarding-house keeper as sub warden, and a number of West Indian, West African, Arab and Jewish men and women as wardens and messengers. Little said, 'The A.R.P. duties in the district in general appear to have brought about quite a strong sense of comradeship and co-operation.' Working at Butetown's 'International Warden's Post' as an ARP warden was Edward Bovell, one of the community's oldest and most respected citizens. Bovell came to Cardiff from Barbados in 1885 and settled in Butetown's Sophia Street. He remembered the race riots of 1919 and long periods of unemployment after the First World War. He worked as a ship's cook until 1940 and then served as a warden in a local ARP post comprising fourteen nationalities.[4] Bovell died in St David's Hospital in Cardiff on 18 February 1961 at the age of 94.

★★★

The bombing of the Cardiff docks began in August 1940, and the air raids intensified with the Cardiff Blitz, which began on 2 January 1941. Some Butetown children had been evacuated, but others stayed with their families. The singer Shirley Bassey, aged 4 at the time of the Cardiff Blitz, recalled in an interview in *Empire News* (19 February 1956):

> Mother always used to lock our bedroom door when we were safely asleep but during the big air raid on the Cardiff docks a bomb blew the windows in. My sisters Grace and Eileen had their faces cut by flying glass and started to scream blue murder. When my mother unlocked the bedroom door, they all scrambled out, leaving me behind, yelling.

Eventually Shirley's sisters and brothers were evacuated to the valleys, 'leaving me at home with my mother. I missed them but as long as I had my mother I was alright.'

Louise Benjamin, who was also raised in Butetown during the war, told Bassey's biographer, John L. Williams:

> We would look out over the Channel to Bristol, watch ack-ack guns firing, you could see it all in the sky. We'd go down to the Esplanade and watch. For my mother, with my father at sea, it must have been horrific, but as a child, that was what life was. After a while my mother got very blasé and we went under the stairs. I can remember one night we went under the stairs and my mother had hold of my hair and every time there was a blast she would pull and I was screaming.[5]

★★★

Len Johnson was known as Manchester's 'Uncrowned King of Boxing'. He was born there to a West African father and an Irish-Mancunian mother. In spite of being acknowledged as one of the finest middleweight boxers of the 1920s and 1930s, Johnson was prevented from fighting for British titles because of his colour. From 22 December 1940, Manchester became the seventh-most heavily bombed city in Britain during the war. At first Len worked as a rescue foreman, but he was later transferred to an ARP centre where he was a member of the heavy rescue squad. Johnson's biographer, Michael Herbert, has shared some of the correspondence he received about Len's war work.

One correspondent, Miss I. Roach, recalled that when Len was in the Manchester Civil Defence, he worked in the rescue squad at the Park Street (West Garden) Depot where she was employed as an ambulance driver. Miss Roach described Len as 'a smashing bloke, friendly with everyone, and liked by everyone'.

Mrs M. Raine remembered that Len loved a game of billiards. 'He was a big man – very kind and gentle and perfectly mannered. We all respected him.' Another correspondent, Neville Robson, was struck by Len's 'gentlemanly demeanour, quite unexpected to me, for a boxer', and described Len's wartime role as a member of the civil defence heavy rescue squad based at the ARP centre in the old school in Claremont Road, Moss Side, south of the city centre:

> My father was superintendent of that Depot and spoke very highly of Len's excellent record. The heavy rescue squad were equipped with mostly old single decker buses, painted grey and with all the old seats taken out, and windows boarded up. These were full of ropes, axes, crowbars, jacks, spades and other equipment and the job was to rescue folk trapped in their houses and other buildings after the bombings which were very heavy in Manchester. Liverpool suffered just as much. Dad used to tell me that Len would work as a 'human dynamo' and would not worry about the tremendous risks he was taking of the building collapsing onto him.

In 1943–44 Len worked as a civil defence instructor in the Civil Defence Reserve (Unit No. 1), which was located at Kent's Bank near Grange-over-Sands, Cumbria. These units were set up by the Ministry of Home Security to meet any unexpected attacks by the German Air Force. Len joined the unit in Cumbria as a specialist in first aid and physical training. Michael Herbert said:

> Obviously his years of training as a boxer and dealing with injuries sustained in the ring had given him a wealth of experience in this area … Len is remembered by other members of the unit as a very sociable person who was well respected by everyone.[6]

★★★

William 'Bill' Miller, the grandson of a freed slave from Sierra Leone, was born in the Devonshire port city of Plymouth and was a Labour councillor and alderman there from the 1920s. As early as 1938, Bill criticised Plymouth City Council's ill-conceived preparations for German air raids. 'There has been muddle, drift and incompetency,' he said.[7] He expressed his concerns that the council were unprepared for bombing raids and he advocated the evacuation of the civilian population. 'It will be essential, for instance, to evacuate the public … There may be an opportunity for getting our people out of all this slaughter.' Bill's concerns were ignored by the council, and he immediately joined the Civil Defence Wardens Service.

Bill's fears were realised after the Fall of France in June 1940. Plymouth was one of the most vulnerable cities on the coastline. As an air-raid warden, Bill organised the evacuation of some local mothers and their children without orders:

> He commandeered buses, lorries and other vehicles and used them to take women and children to safe areas outside the city. The government had not authorised this evacuation. Bill

was arrested for taking the law into his own hands and put on trial … During the trial, he was asked why he had decided to organise the evacuation. He replied that he had told the men in his area who had gone away to fight in the war that he would do his best to protect their wives and families and this was the reason for his actions.[8]

Bill was found guilty by the tribunal. His punishment was a severe warning, but three days later the official evacuation began. Bill felt that this vindicated his actions.

Bill was the head air-raid warden in Stonehouse, one of three towns that was later amalgamated into Plymouth, during the heaviest bombing raids which commenced in March 1941. The city was heavily bombed by the Luftwaffe in a series of raids known as the Plymouth Blitz. Although the dockyards were the principal targets, much of the city centre and over 3,700 houses were destroyed and more than 1,000 civilians lost their lives. Bill's own house in East Street was hit by a bomb in 1941 and he suffered temporary hearing loss as a result. His sister-in-law was severely injured, and his two younger children had slight injuries.

Bill remained head warden in Stonehouse until August 1941, but at a crucial time during the Plymouth Blitz he displayed great dedication and played an important role in the organisation of the warden service. He also persuaded the army to provide field kitchens in the streets to feed the people and obtained the help of the marines in clearing the debris left by the air raids. The air raids left Plymouth devastated: its population was reduced by almost half. Bill's son, Claude, described his father as a very kind and gentle man:

He didn't do anyone any harm. He was respected. A man of the people. You couldn't go for a walk with him in Plymouth because people would stop him and want to talk to him. One of the reasons he isn't better known is that historians take more notice of people from London.[9]

9

Keeping the Home Fires Burning

Entertainers played an important role in raising morale during the Second World War. They performed to the public, troops and munitions factory workers up and down the country. Many of them joined ENSA (the Entertainments National Service Association), an organisation set up in 1939 to provide entertainment for British armed forces personnel. A host of well-known stars took part in ENSA shows, including Gracie Fields, George Formby and Laurence Olivier. Entertainers also made themselves available to the American troops after the USA entered the war in December 1941.

At the outbreak of hostilities, there were many black entertainers and musicians working in Britain. Some of them were American expatriates who could have returned to the USA but preferred to stay in their adopted homeland. By the outbreak of war, many of them had built up a strong relationship with the British public, and some of them were household names. Among the most famous were Leslie Hutchinson (popularly known as 'Hutch'), Elisabeth Welch and Adelaide Hall. In addition to being associated with their appearances in classy West End nightclubs such as the Café de Paris, the wider British public were familiar with these black stars through variety theatres, BBC Radio (see Chapter 12), Radio Luxembourg and, from 1936 until 1939, a new medium called television. They were also among the best-selling recording artistes of the day. These well-loved stars of popular music and entertainment were more than willing to support the British war effort.

In Britain in the 1930s the Grenada-born cabaret entertainer Leslie Hutchinson was popular with the high society world of nightclubs in London's theatrical district of the West End. Fellow cabaret star Elisabeth Welch described him as a very elegant gentleman who enjoyed flirting with the ladies:

> He dressed beautifully in Savile Row suits and carried himself as an Englishman. One of his trademarks was the white handkerchief in his left sleeve. He was a lovely person who put on airs, but we didn't mind because he was having fun as well. He gave the impression that he always woke up with a smile.[1]

Due to the fear of air raids, during the first two weeks of the war, cinemas, theatres, dance halls and other places of public entertainment were closed, but this was a temporary measure. There were no air raids during the first year of the war and gradually places of entertainment reopened for business.

In the third week of the war, Hutch was seen in a variety show at the Birmingham Hippodrome. While Hutch's on-stage contemporaries made fun of Hitler and other Nazi leaders – with the permission of the Lord Chamberlain, the senior officer of the Royal Household with authority over theatre censorship – Hutch preferred to focus on what he did best: singing romantic songs.

In her biography of Hutch, Charlotte Breese acknowledged that his wartime appearances were greatly appreciated by the British public, especially during air raids, and quoted a 'Manchester fan' who remembered, 'The bombing started during his performance, but Hutch just carried on playing the piano and singing, also mopping his brow a usual. He helped us to forget the Blitz for a while … Hutch was a real trouper.'[2]

Hutch was indeed a 'real trouper'. In the middle of an appearance in Glasgow the air-raid siren sounded, but he just shrugged his shoulders, went on singing, and defiantly told the audience after the all-clear went, 'Let's sing our answer to that', and sang 'There'll Always be an England'.

★★★

When Britain declared war on Germany, American citizens were advised by their government to return home, but the expatriate Elisabeth Welch had made London her home. As she explained, 'All my friends were here and I didn't want to leave them.' Elisabeth was born in New York and settled in London in 1933. For six decades she was one of the most popular singers working in Britain and a permanent fixture on the West End musical stage. The British public were drawn to her beauty and elegance, and her soft, lovely voice. Elisabeth regarded herself as American by birth and English in thought and interest. London was her home for seventy years.

When war broke out, Elisabeth joined the first concert party to entertain the forces in Britain. In an unidentified press cutting in her scrapbook, Elisabeth described that first concert (for the Royal Air Force):

> A little hall was packed. Appearing that night were stars like Evelyn Laye, Frances Day and the Western Brothers. Oh, a terrific company. No theatre in the world could afford to hire the lot of us at once. What wonderful appreciation we got! What a thrill we got out of doing it for nothing! We couldn't help having lumps in our throats.

Elisabeth continued to join some of her show business pals to entertain the troops:

A lot of artists would call up friends and get parties together, sometimes with War Office permission. If we went out of London, transport was laid on for us. Wherever we went the boys were very pleased to see us. Sometimes they were a bit stunned, agog at who was up there on the stage in front of them – people like Vivien Leigh, Kay Hammond and Michael Wilding. Often we had no stage. I've been on a truck, with a terrible broken down piano, to sing to about six men on an Ack-Ack site in the middle of nowhere. I don't think they really wanted me to sing – though, as the piano was there, I did – they just wanted somebody to talk to. They were bored, lonely, and tense, waiting for enemy planes to come over.[3]

In November 1942, Elisabeth received a telegram from the War Office asking if she would travel to the overseas territory of Gibraltar to entertain the garrison there in an all-star revue called *Christmas Party*. The show was organised by Hugh 'Binkie' Beaumont of H.M. Tennent's, a well-known theatrical management outfit that made sure its stars played troop shows. The company flew out to Gibraltar on 23 December, and fifty years later Elisabeth recalled in the *Sunday Telegraph*:

Well, what greater compliment could be asked of a foreigner than to join the company of people like Phyllis Stanley, Jeanne de Casalis, Dame Edith Evans, Beatrice Lillie, John Gielgud, and Michael Wilding! I was very proud, and grateful! We were asked by the War Office to go out to Gibraltar to entertain the troops. Not ENSA, but HM [His Majesty's] Government itself, the men with red braid on their caps. I felt very grand. We flew out in a Dutch plane with the windows all blacked out because we weren't supposed to see where we were going. We landed in Lisbon in what looked like a sea of swastikas. Because Portugal was neutral everyone stopped there for repairs and refuelling, and it was quite a shock to step out of the plane and see Nazi planes all round us. We girls gave our own brasshats a shock too. We were all three wearing trousers and they asked us frostily to change, which we did not.[4]

During their four-week stay the company performed fifty-six shows. Most of them were given in the peninsula's Rock Theatre but others included one on board a ship to more than 2,000 men, two in the local hospitals, and some on board battleships and aircraft carriers.

They also toured gun sites, where they talked to the men. Most of the troops had been stationed in Gibraltar for two years and so were a responsive and grateful audience. Elisabeth commented, 'They were very emotional days, especially out there in Gibraltar where the boys were going to be killed and the ships to be sunk. It's hard to sing when your throat tightens up and you are fighting back tears.'[5] John Gielgud described Elisabeth's memorable performance in the May 1943 edition of *Theatre Arts*:

> Elisabeth Welch sings 'Prayer for Rain', 'Begin the Beguine', and 'Solomon', in a black dress against a white satin curtain, and you can hear a pin drop while she is singing, but when she has finished the thunder of applause can be heard in the street.

***

In 1943, three years after she had lost the New Florida club in an air raid on London, Adelaide Hall joined ENSA. One of the first things she did was to have a uniform specially tailored for her by Madame Adele of Grosvenor Street. She said, 'Oh, it was smart! It was sand brown, with a lovely cap, and I had a shirt and tie too. It was a first class uniform but I couldn't stand the collar. It was very stiff.'[6] Adelaide loved the uniform, and wore it with pride whenever and wherever she could.

Adelaide was proud of the fact that she was one of the first entertainers to enter Germany before the war was over. She travelled through Germany for ENSA, appearing in garrison theatres everywhere and, as the war drew to a close, she moved along with the troops:

> It was a very dangerous thing to do, but I didn't think about that. I just did what I had to do. I was on edge, and some-times very frightened, but I persevered. It was hard work but I'm glad I went. I loved it. Sometimes we travelled in our jeeps across the fields in the dark. I had my own jeep and a driver.[7]

When Adelaide arrived at a camp, she would find the hall packed with soldiers:

> The door opened and the place was full of soldiers and smoke. I did my cabaret act and the boys had a ball. Sometimes we didn't have a stage so we had to improvise from the floor. At some of the concerts I sang to thousands of soldiers and it was so moving when they joined in. I shall never forget the time they sang 'Swing Low, Sweet Chariot' with me. They all had different voices. Some were baritones, others sang high, and it was a wonderful thing to hear.

Audiences never forgot Adelaide's contribution to the war effort. Mrs F. Cross remembered Adelaide's performance being inter-rupted by an air raid:

> As we were ATS [Auxiliary Territorial Service] from the gun site in Hyde Park we stayed put as it was an unexpected night off. We thought we would wait till the show started again but it didn't stop. Adelaide sang and sang, the bombs dropped around us, but no one left. She was wonderful.[8]

Jean Brown, who served as a corporal in the Women's Auxiliary Air Force (WAAF) during the Second World War, recalled seeing Adelaide at the Empire Theatre in Newcastle-on-Tyne in 1944:

Adelaide was the star of the show. About six of us were invited to sell programmes at the theatre. Some of the proceeds was for the RAF Benevolent Fund. After a marvellous show, we were asked to go and meet her in the dressing-room. I have never forgotten her, quite a large lady with a beautiful smile. She was wearing a lilac satin evening dress and it was off the shoulder style. She was also wearing lovely earrings which were shaped like small hands and each had a brilliant red stone. I'm thinking rubies and they probably were, but I still have a vivid picture in my memory. She was very sincere and interested in what we were all doing and how we were coping so far from home. I am sorry I've lost my programme as I am sure we could get her autograph. It gives me great pleasure to tell you that I met this wonderful star whose voice could have lifted the roof off.[9]

10

Ivor Cummings

In 1998 Ivor Cummings was described by Mike Phillips and Trevor Phillips in *Windrush: The Irresistible Rise of Multi-Racial Britain* as 'a fastidious, elegant man, with a manner reminiscent of Noel Coward – he chain smoked with a long cigarette holder and addressed visitors as "dear boy"'.[1] However, they did not refer directly to his sexuality. Cummings was gay in an age of hostility, when being homosexual was a criminal offence.[2] He was also one of the most important and influential black men in wartime Britain.

Cummings was born in West Hartlepool, north-east England. His mother was an English nurse and his father a doctor from Sierra Leone. Before the war, in 1935, he found employment as the resident secretary and housekeeper of Aggrey House, a centre for colonial students, mostly from Africa and the West Indies, set up by the government in Bloomsbury.

In conversation with Mike Phillips in the 1970s, Cummings revealed that he had been denied a commission in the armed services at the start of the war because of a rule in the King's Regulations. It stated that HM's officers had to be of pure European descent. This was abandoned shortly after, but by then

Cummings had accepted a post in the Civil Service.[3] His war-time role as the assistant welfare officer for the Colonial Office earned him a reputation as someone who would assist any black person in trouble.

In 1941, as a representative of the Colonial Office, Cummings visited the East End of London to investigate complaints he had received from the representative of a group of African and West Indian merchant seamen and workers from the Beckton Gas Works. In his report of his visit, dated 19 May 1941, Cummings described how, two days earlier, he had travelled to Aldgate and about forty-five men had turned up to the meeting to discuss their problems. Their chief complaints were, in order of impor-tance, that they had no meeting place, which forced them onto the streets night after night, making them vulnerable to police harassment; they faced a 'colour bar' in some air-raid shelters; and the ARP authorities had offered them a separate shelter to them-selves, which was proclaimed to be inferior and vulnerable to bombs. In his report, Cummings stated, 'They seemed very anx-ious that I should see the Chief Warden on the subject, and they urged that I should attend to it at once.'

They also spoke at length about police harassment. The police were very hard on them and would arrest them for trivial offences or incidents. Cummings stressed the need for action and recom-mended a 'thorough discussion' with the British Sailor's Society about the position of African and West Indian seamen in the Port of London, and suggested that some consideration should be given to the provision of a club for the men. 'I considered them a good type and I believe that they would make an excellent Club if they were given the opportunity. Something very modest would do.'

Regarding the discrimination in the air-raid shelters, Cummings proposed to get further evidence before the ARP authorities were approached. Cummings had had previous expe-rience of police harassment when he worked for Aggrey House in the 1930s. 'Complaints reached me that coloured people in the

Tottenham Court Road area were being unduly molested by the police,' he said.

With regard to the situation in 1941, he proposed the same direct action he took in the 1930s. 'I went to the Police Station and brought the matter up before the Superintendent. This had a good effect … Therefore in this matter I think a similar course of action would have the desired effect.' Cummings concluded that the men were 'most anxious for me to visit them again soon … I am very anxious not to lose touch with them.'[4]

In 1948, when Cummings was at Tilbury to meet the passengers embarking from the *Empire Windrush*:

He addressed the migrants in a tone of patronising kindliness which exactly echoed the spirit of the time. 'I now want to address my friends who have nowhere to go and no plans whatsoever. I am afraid you will have many difficulties, but I feel sure that with the right spirit and by cooperating as I have suggested above, you will overcome them.' On the surface he maintained an iron neutrality as befitted a senior Civil Servant. But in conversation with Mike Phillips in the seventies he revealed that, at the time, he was desperately anxious about the migrants' prospects.[5]

11

Learie Constantine

In the 1930s, the Trinidadian Learie Constantine, popularly known as 'Connie', was among the best-paid sportsmen in Britain. As a first-class cricketer he accepted an offer from Nelson, a prominent Lancashire league team, to play for them in a professional capacity. He settled in Nelson in 1929. He played for them for eight seasons until 1937 and made the town his home until 1949. Constantine later reflected on his responsibility as the first black professional cricketer who came to the Lancashire league:

> I had a job to do to satisfy people. I was as human as they were … I had to set an example … I carried a burden but I was helped tremendously by my wife … I felt as a pioneer I had to leave something creditable behind.[1]

When war broke out, Constantine could have taken his wife, Norma, and their young daughter Gloria to the safety of Trinidad, but he believed he owed something to the country that had adopted them. He said:

> I couldn't run away. I had got a standard of life in England that I could never have achieved in my country. I had made a lot of

friends. England to me stood for something and now that war had started I would have felt like a little dog to have run away from England.[2]

The Constantine family stayed.

In Nelson, Constantine helped to prepare the local community for war by sandbagging a local hospital and volunteering as an air-raid equipment officer, although it turned out that Nelson was never bombed. He also accepted a job as a billeting officer. His duties included finding accommodation for servicemen who were stationed in the Nelson area and inspecting and grading local houses in preparation for evacuees from Bradford and Manchester. Though nearly 40, Constantine expected to undertake some form of military service but instead he was offered a job as a Welfare Officer for the Ministry of Labour and National Service, in conjunction with the Colonial Office, in the north-west region of England.

His biographer, Gerald Howat, explained, 'His organisational ability, personal prestige, experience of Lancashire and racial background made him the ideal person to deal with the absorption of West Indians into the Merseyside industrial and social scene'.[3]

It was a fairly senior but temporary Civil Service post. His main wartime role was to look after the interests of African seamen in Liverpool, and munitions workers and trainees from the West Indies in the north-west. Many of them had been hastily recruited from rural areas of the Caribbean. The government needed someone to act on their behalf and Constantine accepted. He was helped by an assistant, Sam Morris, who was active in the LCP.

The work began in October 1941 and Constantine was initially based in Liverpool's famous Royal Liver Building. It was in Liverpool that he experienced wartime bombing, but he was not troubled by the German air raids. 'I was a good sleeper in those days. I'd hear the siren but not the all clear because I had slept all through the bombing!'[4]

In Liverpool a great number of West Indians were employed as welders, tin plate workers and dockers in the Gladstone Docks.

Sometimes, if there were racial tensions, Constantine intervened and mediated. It could be tough and demanding work, but he rose to the challenge:

> I had to do almost everything for them. I had to see they were comfortable in the factory. I had to make arrangements to see that they sent their money home. I had to look into the hostels that housed them while they were here. I had to help them to find digs when they were working in Birkenhead and places like that.[5]

Even though the West Indians had travelled to England to help the war effort, they often faced suspicion, hostility and discrimination in housing, their wages and their working conditions. Another Constantine biographer, Peter Mason, said:

> Most were ill equipped for life in the grey industrial north of wartime England, and at times their demands frustrated Constantine, who, as a hardened settler, found the naivety and niggles of the young immigrants rather taxing … He was though, on the whole, deeply sympathetic to the plight of those he was asked to be an advocate for. They suffered many of the indignities that he had already experienced, yet without the buffer of his unusual status and financial comfort … Although prepared to be outspoken, his preference was for talk rather than outright confrontation, and he was particularly successful in dealing with a strike of African merchant seamen, of whom there were also many based in Liverpool during the war.[6]

Constantine worked tirelessly on the behalf of the West Indian war workers at various levels: with government departments, the LCP, the churches and the United States forces. He also negotiated with trade unions and employers who flatly refused to employ black workers. In 1954, Constantine explained in his book *The Colour Bar* that, during the war, older unions, such as the boilermakers', opposed black workers entering the industry. They said it had been difficult to find places for returning soldiers whose jobs had been taken by temporary workers during the First World War. They did not want the same thing to happen again. However, Constantine acknowledged that the electrical unions were more co-operative and black members took places on their union committees. Then there were those firms that either flatly refused to employ black workers:

> … or put endless delays in their way hoping to make them seek work elsewhere. I used to get the Ministry to press those firms for most urgent deliveries of orders, and then they found that they must take some coloured workers or get none of any kind. With urgent work to be done, they were forced to give way.[7]

On other occasions, Constantine had to negotiate with some white hostel residents when they objected to sharing their accommodation with black workers. Once, Constantine took a private room in one of the hostels so that 'the white workers could see that I was an ordinary person like themselves and then might be willing to try some other coloured people as acquaintances'.[8]

However, though the experiment proved successful, while staying at the hostel Constantine ran into trouble one evening when he joined some friends at the dance hall. An American Air Force officer shouted at him to get out of the hall, 'We don't allow n****** to mix with white people where we are.' When Constantine politely asked the man to go away, the American replied, 'Get out n*****, before I smash you.' Constantine came close to hitting the American but realised that the newspaper headlines would have inflamed the situation, as well as the hostility directed at West Indian workers and servicemen from some white American troops. Peter Mason said:

> He always preferred a mannered response rather than an off-the-cuff aggressive reaction, reasoning that it worked better to

portray the aggressor as undignified and unreasoning – to show that it was the perpetrator who was the sad victim of racism, not himself … Sam Morris said that while most [West Indians] paid him the greatest respect as an understanding elder brother figure, some were sceptical … of his genuineness and dubbed him a black Englishman.[9]

Constantine made regular wartime broadcasts for the BBC to the Caribbean in programmes like *Calling the West Indies* and to listeners in Britain. However, in 1943, when he submitted a script about racism in Britain to G.R. Barnes, who was the BBC's director of talks, it was rejected. Barnes considered it 'too controversial' for a series called *Sunday Postscript*. Barnes then added that he would accept the script for a weekday broadcast if Constantine and the Colonial Office passed it.[10]

During the war, he took part in a couple of important documentary film shorts, made for propaganda purposes: *West Indies Calling* (1943) and *Learie Constantine* (1944) (see Chapter 21). He gave lectures to the forces, made hospital visits and played in charity cricket matches. Through his work as a community leader and broadcaster, Constantine was one of the most famous, respected and influential black men in Britain in the war years. However, his position did not protect him from an act of overt racism he experienced with his family in 1943.

There was to be an international cricket match at Lord's Cricket Ground on 2 August and Constantine was given special leave from his war duties to take part. On arriving in London with his wife and daughter on 30 July, Constantine and his family were refused entry to the Imperial Hotel in Russell Square. The hotel feared that American guests would object to having black guests among them. The historian David Killingray explained:

On arrival at the hotel he was told in insulting terms by the woman manager that 'we will not have n****** in the hotel because of the Americans' … The interests of racially prejudiced white customers were then commonly used as an excuse to exclude non-white people from hotels, restaurants, and dances.[11]

Constantine took the hotel to court and he won the much-publicised court case, *Constantine versus Imperial Hotel, London* (1944).[12] However, many other black people were not so fortunate when they complained of racism in the forces and factories. Giving judgement to the Constantine case, Mr Justice Birkett described the hotel manageress as a 'lamentable figure in the witness box … She was grossly insulting in her reference to Mr Constantine, and her evidence is unworthy of credence.' He added that Constantine 'bore himself with modesty and dignity, and dealt with questions with intelligence and truth'.[13]

In spite of the problems he encountered, when he was interviewed on BBC Television for *Calypso for Constantine* in 1966, he spoke positively about the war years:

All the people in England had a comradeship which you wouldn't be able to appreciate now. Everybody was one. Everybody was smiling in the face of adversity. I just wish we could recapture that spirit in England.[14]

12

The BBC

It could be argued that, in wartime, the British Broadcasting Corporation (BBC) was, for the most part, a colour-blind organisation. Its television service was abandoned for the duration of the war, but radio continued and created a sense of national cohesion that followed the BBC's principles of providing first-rate information, education and entertainment. This allowed the whole nation, as well as citizens of the empire, to feel included through voices rather than vision. However, from time to time, racist language and racial stereotypes did surface and these were challenged by leaders in Britain's black community, such as Dr Harold Moody.

During the war, the BBC provided both news and entertainment for its listeners, at home and overseas. In music programmes, a diverse range of black vocalists, who lent themselves to the intimacy of radio broadcasting, included Elisabeth Welch, Leslie 'Hutch' Hutchinson, Evelyn Dove, Turner Layton, Ida Shepley and Adelaide Hall. They were regularly employed by the BBC in various popular music and variety shows and these included *Monday Night at Eight*, *Variety Bandbox*, *Starlight* and *Workers' Playtime*. They could be heard on the Home Service, Light Programme, Third Programme and the Forces Network. They also took part in programmes made for the colonies on the BBC's Empire Service, such as *Calling the West Indies* and *Calling West Africa*.

In 1943 Adelaide Hall had her own series *Wrapped in Velvet* on the Forces Network. In May 1945, during the Victory in Europe celebrations, the African American entertainer Josephine Baker visited London and took part in several victory shows and BBC broadcasts. In fact, throughout the war, black musicians and entertainers could be heard in a range of morale-boosting music shows. Additionally, well-known black actors were given leading roles in dramatic programmes.

However, in 1940 Dr Harold Moody complained to the BBC after a radio announcer had used the word 'n★★★★★' during a broadcast. In a written statement to Dr Moody dated 16 May 1940, the BBC admitted liability for the presenter's comments, and offered a full apology.[1] In 1942 Dr Moody wrote a letter of protest to the director general of the BBC after the exclusion of Africans and West Indians from their radio programme *Good Night to the Forces*.

It is likely that Dr Moody also complained about the blackface minstrel tradition which was adapted for BBC Radio in 1933 in the popular series *The Kentucky Minstrels*. It ran successfully until 1950, but *The Kentucky Minstrels'* promotion of 'Old South' racist stereotypes co-existed alongside more progressive and honest images of black people. For example, in 1944 BBC Radio helped to launch the British career of the Trinidadian folk singer Edric Connor in programmes like *Travellers' Tales*. His widow, Pearl, also from Trinidad, later said:

> The BBC was interested in helping to promote and assist some of the third-world people, and the Caribbean people. So Edric came to Britain at a good time. Doors were open to him. He didn't have to kick too hard. There was an open-door policy. They weren't locking us out yet. [In the 1940s] Edric became a major celebrity on BBC Radio, and a much-loved and respected ambassador for the arts and culture of the Caribbean.[2]

Edric's introduction to radio listeners in 1944 coincided with a landmark year for black artistes on the airwaves. Edric played Joe and sang 'Old Man River' in *Show Boat*; Robert Adams took the lead in Eugene O'Neill's *The Emperor Jones* and in a *Children's Hour* presentation he portrayed the African American leader Booker T. Washington; and Elisabeth Welch starred in an adaptation of George Bernard Shaw's short story, *The Adventures of the Black Girl in Her Search for God*.

However, in 1944, one of the most innovative drama productions broadcast on BBC Radio was *The Man Who Went to War*. Three of America's most famous black actors, Paul Robeson, Canada Lee and Ethel Waters, participated in this historic BBC Radio production, which they recorded in New York. Robeson spoke the prologue in this 'ballad opera' written by the African American Langston Hughes. Canada Lee and Ethel Waters played the leads. It was first broadcast in America on 20 February 1944, and then in Britain on 6 March (from records made from the American broadcast). The cast was brought together in New York, where Robeson was appearing on the Broadway stage in *Othello*, by one of the BBC's top radio producers, D.G. Bridson. He recalled in his autobiography:

My plan was to write a simple sort of folk-tale round the lives of a man and his wife in a town like London during the war. But though their story would be London's own, the town itself – like the man and his wife – would not be English, but Negro. The man joins up and goes to fight the war with his friends; his wife goes to work in a war factory and suffers all the terrors of the Blitz…The impact of the work in performance was incredibly moving. Ethel Waters' parting from her husband and her singing of *Sometimes I Feel Like a Motherless Child* almost stopped the show in the studio … As a gesture of friendship from one people to another, *The Man Who Went to War* was probably unique. As a prophetic echo of the Negro's post-war struggle for Civil Rights, it might have been a timely warning.

Either way, it was quite one of the most popular broadcasts I ever had on the air, being heard in Britain by nearly ten million listeners on its first transmission alone.[3]

For listeners who appreciated classical music, there was a programme dedicated to the black British composer Samuel Coleridge-Taylor on the Home Service in 1942. His best-known composition was *The Song of Hiawatha*, a trilogy of cantatas written between 1898 and 1900. In the programme his daughter, Avril, was engaged to conduct several of his compositions with the BBC Orchestra.

That same year, also on the Home Service, in *Military Band*, *Three African Dances* by Montague Ring (the pseudonym of British-born Amanda Ira Aldridge) was played. This was a rare example of a black woman composer being acknowledged by the BBC. In 1944, the Nigerian composer Fela Sowande had his *African Suite* broadcast on the BBC's Home Service.

There was another momentous occasion on 28 September 1943 when BBC Radio broadcast a particular concert live from the Royal Albert Hall in London. Organised by the United States Army, it featured a choir of 200 African American soldiers, then stationed in Britain. The concert, which the BBC broadcast on their Forces Network, had been prepared by the composer Marc Blitzstein, an openly gay Jew from Philadelphia. He was also a communist and a corporal in the military, having joined the US Eighth Army Air Force.

Blitzstein composed 'Freedom Morning' for the occasion because he had been incensed about the blatant oppression and segregation of African American GIs in Britain. 'Freedom Morning' was introduced by the choir. The African American tenor Roland Hayes travelled across the Atlantic to take part and sing spirituals as he had in 1921 at Buckingham Palace for King George V and Queen Mary. Hayes also sang arias by Bach and Arne.

★★★

There was one programme made by the BBC during the war that did not make it onto the airwaves. In June 1943 a discussion programme about racism in Britain called *The Colour Bar* was recorded but not broadcast. Hosted by the anthropologist Kenneth Little, three black guests openly discussed their experiences of racism. The speakers were Aduke Alakija, a West African woman who was studying social science at Cambridge University; community leader Dr Harold Moody; and the actor Robert Adams.

The guests highlighted the mistreatment many Africans and West Indians faced when they arrived in Britain. Some encountered problems in finding accommodation, and Adams emphasised that 'colour prejudice is fairly general in this country'. After listening to the recording, G.R. Barnes, the BBC's director of talks, recommended that *The Colour Bar* be broadcast in the evening but suggested that the peak listening time of 9.20 p.m. be avoided for fear of 'exacerbating an already heated issue'. Barnes noted that the programme should be considered 'a conversation between friends'.

However, during a weekly meeting with the Colonial Office, it became apparent that there had been an increasing number of complaints from black people about racism and discrimination in wartime Britain. The Colonial Office looked favourably on *The Colour Bar* and hoped that it would bring 'the whole subject [of race] out into the light of day'.

Then Barnes had a change of heart. He was concerned that a discussion programme about racism 'was apt to deal in generalities and abstract questions which were often beyond ordinary men and women' in Britain. He recommended to the Home Service that they not broadcast the programme. He 'very much regretted the decision' and insisted that the guests receive payment for their contributions. He also requested that the script be filed 'in case usage could be made of it at a later date'.[4]

Dr Harold Moody.
(Author's collection)

A young evacuee
leaving London in
1940. (Courtesy of the
Imperial War Museum:
Ref. HU 55936)

Adelaide Hall and
Fela Sowande at the
New Florida Club
in 1940. (Author's
collection)

From left to right:
Dora Plaskitt, Kathy
Joyce (the author's
mother) and Esther
Bruce in 1942.
(Author's collection)

Fireman George A. Roberts. Portrait by Norman Hepple, 1941. (Courtesy of the estate of Norman Hepple/ Bridgeman Images)

Fernando Henriques (top row, with the beard) with fellow members of the Auxiliary Fire Service in Hampstead, London. (Courtesy of the Imperial War Museum: Ref. D5544)

Earl Cameron.
(Author's collection)

Ken 'Snakehips'
Johnson. (Courtesy
of Peter Powell)

Elisabeth Welch. (Author's collection)

Una Marson and Learie Constantine broadcasting for the BBC's Empire Service in 1942. (Courtesy of the BBC)

Princess Ademola, who worked as a nurse at Guy's Hospital during the Second World War. (Author's collection)

Sergeant Lincoln Lynch from Jamaica. He volunteered for service in the RAF in 1942. (Courtesy of Getty Images)

Two bomber air crew, Sergeant Dickinson (Canada) and Sergeant Leslie Francis Gilkes (Trinidad), wait to board their aircraft for a raid on Hamburg, Germany in 1943. Sergeant Gilkes was killed in action on 3 August 1943. (Courtesy of the Imperial War Museum: Ref. PL 10348D)

Pilot Officer John Smythe being shown how to use the sextant by an instructor in 1943. (Courtesy of the Imperial War Museum: Ref. CH 10740)

Flight Lieutenant Ulric Cross DSO, DFC, pictured after receiving his decorations at Buckingham Palace in 1945. (Courtesy of the Imperial War Museum: Ref. HU 58315)

Ramsay and Lilian Bader in 1943. (Courtesy of Lilian Bader)

Norma Quaye with fellow members of the Auxiliary Territorial Service in 1939. (Courtesy of Getty Images)

A group of West Indian Auxiliary Territorial Service (ATS) recruits recently arrived at their training camp in 1943. (Courtesy of Getty Images)

Paul Robeson in *The Proud Valley* (1940). (Author's collection)

African and Caribbean War Memorial in Windrush Square, Brixton,
London. (Author's collection)

13

Una Marson

Una Marson was a Jamaican feminist, poet, playwright and social activist who came to Britain in 1932. On her arrival she was helped by Dr Harold Moody (see Chapter 3) and his wife, who gave her lodgings in their home in Peckham, as well as a job. For several years she worked as secretary to the LCP. Before long she became well known in London for campaigning on black women's issues, such as discrimination in the nursing profession. At that time, black women who wanted to work as nurses were not welcome in British hospitals.

The July–September 1934 edition of the newsletter of the LCP, known as *The Keys*, published a report from the *News-Chronicle* (15 June 1934) about a young black woman who came to Britain to train as a nurse. She was rejected by all of the twenty-eight hospitals she applied to. The newsletter also reported that LCP member Una had addressed the British Commonwealth Conference in London and informed them:

> No hospital, however, will willingly admit that there is a ban against coloured nurses, but after talking to a number of hospital matrons, secretaries, and governors I learned that a coloured

girl has a very poor chance of securing a nursing post in the average hospital.

The newsletter continued:

Several hospital officials admitted that while they had no objections to coloured nurses, they had to consider the feelings of patients who might strongly object. One secretary said: 'While we have no official colour ban, no coloured girl would stand an earthly chance of becoming a nurse with us.'

Una's activism led to some exceptions being made and these included Princess Tsehai, the daughter of Haile Selassie, the exiled Emperor of Ethiopia. The princess trained as a nurse at London's Great Ormond Street Hospital for Sick Children. The children loved her and, after graduating as a State Registered Nurse on 25 August 1939, she served in London during the Blitz.

An exception was also made for the Nigerian Princess Ademola who came to Britain before the war to train at Guy's Hospital. The princess was the daughter of the Alake of Abeokuta, the paramount chief of Northern Nigeria, and she had journeyed with him to England in 1937 to attend the coronation of King George VI. The chief decided that his daughter should train as a nurse in Britain and specialise in midwifery. At Guy's Hospital she qualified as a State Registered Nurse and remained in London for at least part of the war.

Una's campaigning work in the 1930s led to more West African and Caribbean women travelling to the mother country in wartime to train as nurses. Keen to broaden her horizons, in 1939 Una accepted an offer from Cecil Madden, a BBC producer, to undertake some freelance work on his popular television magazine show, *Picture Page*. This work gave Una a stepping stone into the organisation. The outbreak of war then gave her the opportunity to work for BBC Radio. Consequently, she became the corporation's first black woman programme maker and presenter.

Una's pioneering work for radio spanned just over five years, from April 1940 to December 1945. During a trial period, Una took part in broadcasts about West Indians and the war effort. These included *The Empire at War* (1 April 1940). She ended one of these broadcasts with the following morale-boosting statement, 'I am trying to keep the flag flying for dear old Jamaica in my own way here'.[1]

On 3 March 1941, Una was appointed as full-time programme assistant on the BBC's Empire Service, which had been launched in December 1932. Its broadcasts were mainly aimed at English speakers in the outposts of the British Empire. In April 1941, an article in *London Calling*, the overseas journal of the BBC, announced Una's appointment as a member of staff. It described her background and brought home to overseas readers the realities of London in wartime, and how it was impacting on the broadcaster, 'She has had the experience of having her house fired by one of Hitler's incendiary bombs, and her spare time is taken up as an air-raid shelter marshal in Hampstead.'[2]

Through the weekly series, *Calling the West Indies*, Una was able to send messages from servicemen and women in England to their families and friends back home. Listeners throughout the Caribbean would gather in front of their radios, sometimes up to three times a week, and wait for the programme to begin. Personal messages were broadcast as part of a show alongside popular songs, calypsos and swing music. Guests included many well-known black celebrities of the day, including Ken 'Snakehips' Johnson, Learie Constantine and Elisabeth Welch. In spite of the air raids and other wartime dangers, Una and her guests broadcast from a BBC studio in London and, although it was dangerous, Una understood the importance and value of *Calling the West Indies*.

In addition to her work at the BBC, Una took care of many West Indians, providing accommodation in her home, as well as using it as a meeting place where they could get together and socialise. In *Jamaica Journal*, Erika Smilowitz said, 'Her crowded flat in Bayswater became a meeting spot for West Indian servicemen stationed all over England … Always there was Una's sense of humour dominating the party; she loved to talk and laugh.'[3] Una was very conscious of the struggles faced by West Indians in Britain at that time, and on radio she 'had a knack of infusing her broadcasts with the personal as well as having a sense of the literary and the cultural'.[4]

Towards the end of 1942, Una took part in George Orwell's series, *Voice*. This enabled poets and novelists to read their work straight into the microphone. Consequently, Una devised her own literary programme, clearly based on Orwell's format, and in 1943 she transformed a segment of *Calling the West Indies* into *Caribbean Voices*, which ran until 1958.

In the West Indies the school curriculum was British. Students studied Shakespeare, Dickens, Keats and Yeats. No black West Indian writers were acknowledged, and no one was encouraged to write in Jamaican patois. *Caribbean Voices* helped to change this. It proved to be a landmark series because at that time very few poets and playwrights from the West Indies had been published. The series gave them opportunities to raise their profile – and earn some money. It is now recognised as the single most important literary catalyst for both creative and critical writings in the Caribbean.[5]

Una's biographer Delia Jarrett-Macauley said:

The racial isolation, pride and wartime zeal which characterise Una's war poems would not have been the qualities the BBC was seeking. 'Convoy' is a narrative poem describing a walk during which she sees a truck convoy, lets it pass and observes that every man on board waves to her.[6]

Every man on board who waves to Una is black. 'The Convoy' was published in the April 1945 issue of the LCP's *News Letter*.[7]

'The Convoy'

Then each driver turned to greet me
As his truck went roaring by,
Brightly smiled or waiving gaily
As he quickly caught my eye.

There I stood, moved, yet unmoving,
Weeping with no sign of tears,
Greeting all these unknown soldiers
I had known a thousand years.

For they were my own blood brothers,
Brown like me, as warm of heart,
And their souls were glad to greet me
In the great white busy mart.

Our gay hearts grown sad and wiser
Stirred to life a second then,
A thousand words unsaid, were spoken –
And we each took heart again.

Oh my brothers, in the conflict
Of our own bewildered life,
How much strength we bring each other,
What fine courage for the strife.

14

Royal Air Force

On 19 October 1939 the British Government announced that, for the duration of the war, they would lift the ban that excluded black recruits from the armed services. However, a colour bar remained in place in the RAF until November 1940, when the Air Ministry informed the Colonial Office that it would accept black aircrew candidates from the colonies.

The campaigning work of Dr Harold Moody and others had paid off, but recruitment from the colonies did not begin until after the Battle of Britain in 1940. Mr Fairweather, a Jamaican who joined the RAF in 1943, commented at the age of 92 in 2019:

> England did not stand alone at war. The Caribbean was behind her and other countries of the Commonwealth. It annoys me when you see all the war films that make it look as if the Americans alone won the war. The Americans didn't come into the war until 1942![1]

On 18 June 1940, Winston Churchill warned the British people that 'the whole might and fury of our enemy must very soon turn against us'. Less than one month later, on 10 July, Nazi Germany's air force began to make the first serious air attacks from across the Channel. The Battle of Britain had begun but the RAF successfully defended the country.

However, before British victory, 1,023 aircraft were destroyed. From an estimated crew of 3,000 around half survived the four-month battle. A total of 544 Fighter Command pilots and crew were among the dead, as were more than 700 from Bomber Command and nearly 300 from Coastal Command. The loss of so many RAF personnel during the Battle of Britain made it possible for black recruits to volunteer and join up. They included Cy Grant from British Guiana:

> I was one of the first four people who joined the RAF from the colonies. They had just changed their policy towards recruiting black people, so that's how I got in. I trained as a pilot but then, half way through my training, I was switched to navigator. I didn't make anything of this at the time, because I did not realise that it was not above board. But, much later, I discovered through a friend that there were problems with the English aircrew not wanting to fly with black pilots.[2]

Cy was posted to 103 Squadron at RAF Elsham Wolds in Lincolnshire and joined a mixed Canadian and British seven-man crew of a Lancaster bomber. He qualified as navigator and astronomical navigator on 5 February 1943. He later said, although it was almost impossible for a black recruit to be a pilot, he never experienced any racism in the RAF:

> A war was on and I was wearing a uniform. People were generally friendly. In the streets I occasionally heard a child say, 'Look, mummy, a black man!' That always brought me up sharp. Before coming to England I didn't think of myself as black – a quite salutary shock! I was to realize that I was defined in a certain way 'at home' and another in the 'mother

country'. Coming to terms with either label was to realize that I was an outsider – that white people excluded people of any colour other than their own. On walking into a saloon bar in the country, suddenly there would be a deathly hush. It was as though I had suddenly come from an alien planet. Later, as an officer, there was a mild raising of eyebrows when I first walked into the mess, but this soon turned to acceptance when I spoke the King's English, albeit with my West Indian accent.[3]

In 1941 around 250 Trinidadians travelled to Britain to serve in the RAF but fifty-two were killed in action. Ulric Cross (see Introduction) was one of the 250. He survived the war, in spite of flying on eighty bombing missions to Germany and occupied France. He has been described as the highest ranking and one of the most distinguished West Indian airmen in the Second World War. He was awarded the DFC in June 1944 and the Distinguished DSO in November 1944.

Ulric volunteered for the RAF after witnessing the defeat of the British at Dunkirk in 1940 and saw that the Nazis were continuing to gain power across Europe. He started his training at RAF Cranwell at Sleaford in Lincolnshire. Among the skills he learnt were wireless operation, meteorology, bomb aiming, navigation and Morse code. After he graduated as a pilot officer, Ulric was assigned to Bomber Command, serving as a navigator in 139 (Jamaica) Squadron.[4] Ulric was the only West Indian in 139 Squadron, though it was cosmopolitan and included Polish, Indians, English, Welsh, Scottish, Scandinavians and Dutch aircrew.

When the RAF realised that 80 per cent of their bombs missed their targets, they established a Pathfinder Force to guide the bombers. Ulric joined them:

We dropped flares over the target and bombers coming after us would then bomb our flares. There were about a dozen Pathfinders followed by hundreds of bombers. Sometimes when we dropped our flares the Germans would then drop decoy markers fifty miles away. To combat that we were told to drop our bombs at a particular time, with just a ten-second leeway either side. Punctuality was essential to the job. I did eighty operational flights over Germany, including twenty-one to Berlin. We never had guns; we depended for our safety on accurate navigation and speed. You can't be trained not to be afraid but trained to conquer fear. It comes from a belief that what you're doing is right and is worthwhile. All your flight you are busy, busy, busy. The pilot has more time to be afraid than you do. But when the flak starts coming at you and you are 'coned' in a searchlight you feel fear. But your job is to get to the target on time and that is what you are preoccupied with.[5]

Ulric said that one of the biggest dangers was being 'coned' in a searchlight when the German fighters were around:

If you can't get out of the light you watch for fighters. I was once coned for fifteen minutes going to Berlin. The search-lights light up the whole sky. You can't see yourself lit up but you can see other aircraft in cones. They all look silver what-ever their actual colour. It's amazing. They really stand out. You can be seen for miles around by fighters and flak. My plane was hit by flak many times.

Reflecting on his experiences of wartime Britain for Mike Phillips and Trevor Phillips' book *Windrush*, Ulric said:

We were treated very well, people were welcoming. One thing is we were in uniform. And the whole atmosphere was very dif-ferent … People were curious, children would stop you. Almost impossible to walk through a village without children stopping you to ask you the time, and you knew they merely wanted to hear you speak. I was lucky. I crash landed I think five or six, seven times … the strange thing is that when you're really young you feel immortal. That may well be a defence mechanism, but you do feel immortal, and you knew that obviously the possibility existed, that every time you got up in an aeroplane and flew over Germany you wouldn't come back. That possibility always existed. But the young feel they will live forever ... And I felt I was doing the right thing in trying to stop Hitler. I never felt I was going to the aid of the mother country. Some people did but I would say the majority of us didn't. Reasons differ, but certainly for myself, you're young, this was a tremendous adventure and you were doing it for the right reasons.[6]

★★★

In the 1948 Summer Olympics, held in London, Arthur Wint made history by winning Jamaica's first Olympic gold medal, for running the 400m. Known as the 'Gentle Giant', Wint had served with the RAF during the war. In her biography of him, Wint's daughter, Valerie, said that in wartime, 'He stood tall, elegant, distinguished in his RAF Flight Lieutenant's uniform':

It was powder blue with the Wings on the left breast denoting a pilot. His cap sat at a jaunty angle, slanting down to the right. With his exceptionally long legs, he strode along the Strand in London, heading towards the West India Committee offices to collect his mail or to meet his brothers and other friends. He gazed over the heads of most people, while civilians as well as other service men and women regarded him with curiosity. They'd seen many service men and women of colour – they'd come from the Caribbean, from India, to help the Mother Country fend off the Germans, but they had never seen a black officer. They were not sure what to make of him. He, however, was not fazed by their curiosity. He walked through them secure in his personal power and strength.[7]

★★★

Billy Strachan, who also came from Jamaica, had only recently left school and taken a job with the Civil Service when he saw the war as an adventure which would permit him to fly aeroplanes. Billy had no idea how difficult this was going to be. He visited the British Army base in Jamaica and told them that he wanted to join the RAF:

> I had a medical, and was passed fully fit because of my athleticism and sporting activities. A friend of mine, a Jamaican white, went with me. We both passed fit. So we then said to the British Army: 'Right. We want to join. Will you send us to England?' We were laughed out: 'You find your own way there!' We thought they would welcome us, two young, healthy volunteers. So how was I going to get out of Jamaica to get to England?[8]

Billy sold his bicycle and saxophone to pay for his fare to Britain. In March 1940 he arrived in Bristol and then took the train to Paddington Station. Billy attempted to join the RAF by heading straight for the head office of the Air Ministry at a place called Adastral House at the foot of Aldwych. On his arrival he approached a corporal, who Billy thought was the head of the RAF, and was told in no uncertain terms to 'piss off!'. Billy persisted until a sergeant intervened and informed Billy that he could not join the RAF at the Air Ministry. He would have to go to a recruiting station.

After twelve weeks of basic military training he became a wireless operator and air gunner. In 1941 he joined a squadron of Wellington bombers, which made nightly raids over heavily defended German industrial cities. Billy survived thirty operations.

★★★

Eddie Martin Noble was born in Kingston, Jamaica. By the middle of 1941 he was travelling the island as a sales representative. He continued with this until joining the RAF in 1943. It was Noel Coward's patriotic film *In Which We Serve* that inspired Eddie to join up. He later recalled in his autobiography:

> From the moment I saw the film *In Which We Serve*, I had made up my mind that no self-respecting able-bodied young man could honourably remain at home when the fate of the world was literally at stake in Europe.[9]

At the start of the war there was no recruitment in the West Indies for the war effort. In Patrick Vernon's documentary film *A Charmed Life* (2009), Eddie recalled:

> After I came to England I found that the reason for this is that the Prime Minister, Winston Churchill, objected to black men serving alongside white men on equal terms. But a number of English businessmen in the West Indies wanted to make a contribution to the war effort and they decided they would pay for young men to come to England to volunteer for the air force. The experiment was such a success that the colonial governors in the West Indies brought pressure to bear on the Colonial Office. So, Churchill and the government in England was forced to change their attitude and they started recruitment in the West Indies but it had to be voluntary recruitment. And I volunteered.

Eddie felt that he was treated exactly the same as any other airman, except when he went out with white women. Then he faced objections from white servicemen. However, in *A Charmed Life*, he referred to the problems faced by West Indian recruits when they tried for promotion:

> By the end of the war there were 10,000 of us in the RAF, but 99.9% of us never went beyond the rank of sergeant. The Air Ministry would not admit it. A [white] LAC [leading aircraftman] was working under me. I was a Corporal then and I trained him. And we both sat for an examination that would

have moved us to officer cadets. He passed. I failed. I trained him. I know my colour was the reason but no one would admit it.

In 1944 Allan Wilmot, who was also born in Kingston, Jamaica, successfully transferred from the Royal Navy to the Marine Section of the RAF for motorboat duty. He said that there was no official racial discrimination in the services but agreed with Eddie Martin Noble that 'seniority promotion for a black serviceman was rare, even though you were qualified for the job. They didn't want black personnel in charge of white servicemen.'[10]

Allan also acknowledged that white civilians treated black servicemen and women very well. It was appreciated that they had left their homelands to face danger and help Britain in her hour of need. But Allan did not get along with white American GIs:

> They were reluctant to accept the fact that the British black servicemen were a different race in social outlook. Many of the white American GIs were from the Southern states of America and, although they were in Europe, a very different social scene, they couldn't face the changes that took place. So we had open wars, especially in dance halls and various places of entertainment, with the local whites as back-up on our side. The black American GIs were a different story. We got along very well indeed. British black servicemen were their protectors. At times they were attacked by groups of white GIs, especially if they were in the company of white girls. If they attempted to defend themselves against the white GIs, the American police were always at hand to arrest the black ones for the stockade, so we would go to their rescue and try to prevent them from being arrested. Because the American police had no jurisdiction over British servicemen, we could defend them – and ourselves – until the British police arrived on the scene, along with the ambulance for the wounded.

★★★

Nigeria's Babatunde O. Alakija was the first African to be selected for training as a pilot in the RAF. However, in 1941, Peter Thomas became the first African to be granted a commission.[11] Peter, or 'Deniyi' as he was known to his friends, was born in Lagos, Nigeria. In 1940, after reading about the heroic achievements of the RAF in the Battle of Britain, Peter volunteered. He was supported by Charles Woolley, the chief secretary to the government in Nigeria, who personally forwarded Peter's application to London.

Peter set sail for Britain and arrived in Liverpool on 2 May 1941. He was commissioned in mid-1942. *The Times* acknowledged that he was 'the first West African to be commissioned in the RAF and the first to qualify as a pilot'.[12]

Besides the RAF, Peter's interests extended to social welfare and labour problems, and he undertook other responsibilities on behalf of the Colonial Office. He is remembered by Roy Sloan in *Wings of War Over Gwynedd* as 'an interesting and somewhat unusual character':

> He was the son of an extremely wealthy Nigerian dignitary, and was believed to be the only Nigerian flying with the RAF at the time. Thomas was an engaging and attractive personality, well liked and popular with his colleagues, and was exceptionally religious. Normally courteous and gentlemanly, he would let himself go at social events such as Mess parties after being persuaded to take a few drinks and would demonstrate African dances in a most impressive manner.[13]

Sloan noted, however, that Peter 'had a tendency to be involved in mishaps and accidents rather more frequently than one would have expected. It was rumoured that whenever he "bent" an aircraft his father would always foot the bill.'

On 12 January 1945, on a routine exercise over the Brecon Beacons in South Wales, Peter was forced to make a crash landing in the mountains. His companion, a young airman called Frank Stokes, later described what happened:

I glanced up and could clearly see the mountain looming directly ahead of us, as pilot Thomas continued his urgent and ultimately futile attempts to climb. The port wing struck a rocky outcrop and the aircraft slewed to the left, coming to rest on a relatively flat patch of ground; I was rendered unconscious. On coming to, I discovered I was still in my seat, lying on my side. My shins were lacerated and my right eye and bridge of nose were. I had also received a compression fracture of two spinal vertebrae, but did not know about that until much later. I was not wearing my seat belt, as it was usual to undo the lap strap when airborne![14]

Frank then discovered that Peter had been thrown forward, clear of the aircraft:

He was lying on his back, unconscious, breathing heavily with blood oozing from his nose. He was a heavy man, but I managed with some difficulty to turn him onto his side so that his air passages were less likely to become blocked. I then had the idea to try and wrap him in my parachute canopy for warmth, but as I pulled the ripcord, the canopy filled quickly and the strong wind carried it away. I simply didn't have the strength to hold it. It was getting very late in the afternoon, and I decided I could not afford to hang around any longer, or we would both perish from exposure to the elements if not our injuries. Thoughts of happier times passed through my mind as I looked at the desolation all around me. All I could see was the snow-covered mountaintop.

In spite of his injuries, Frank made a painful and difficult descent and managed to stagger over 2 miles in the snow. Eventually he could see the road which led from the Brecon Beacons to Merthyr Tydfil. When he reached it, he discovered he was close to a youth hostel. Luckily there was a warden in residence, who was able to flag down a passing motorist who took Frank to the hospital in Merthyr Tydfil. Before he was treated for the effects of shock and had his leg and facial wounds stitched and dressed, Frank gave directions to the scene of the crash, hoping that Peter would be found. When two senior RAF officers visited Frank to conduct a preliminary investigation, he learned that Peter had not survived the crash. Frank remained in hospital for several weeks, and was visited by Peter's sister:

> … which was very kind of her considering the grief and anguish she must have been experiencing at the tragic loss of her brother. Perhaps she wanted to make sense of her brother's death or just meet someone who had been the last person to see him alive. She may have believed I had spoken with him after the crash, but that had not been possible as he was in a deep state of unconsciousness. She was an intelligent, perceptive woman, an undergraduate at Newcastle Upon Tyne University. I told her what I could about events and she went on her way. There was no further communication between us.

15

Prisoners of War

One of the earliest identified black POWs is Ransford Boi, a seaman in the British merchant fleet who was captured off the coast of Liberia in December 1939. Transferred to the Stalag XB camp at Sandbostel between Bremen and Hanover, he spent two years there before moving to another unnamed internment camp where there were about thirty other black inmates.

Cyril Roberts, the son of the London fireman George A. Roberts (see Chapter 7), was captured at Dunkirk and remained a POW in Germany's Stalag 383 until he was liberated in 1944. Another prisoner of war was the Jamaican-born Patrick Nelson. A gay man, he had worked as a gentleman's valet before he became an artist's model. In 1938 he met the Bloomsbury Group artist Duncan Grant and they began a relationship.

Two years later, Patrick enlisted in the Auxiliary Military Pioneer Corps and went to France with the British Expeditionary Force (BEF). When the Allied forces were evacuated from Dunkirk in May and June 1940, Patrick was injured in the fighting and captured by the Germans. Patrick remained a POW for the next four years.[1]

The stories of black women who were interned are much harder to find. In *Rosie's War – An Englishwoman's Escape from Occupied France* (2011), Rosemary Say recalled her friendship in 1941 with Ronka, a Nigerian. Say briefly described her as 'tall, beautiful, haughty and silent'. Ronka was one of the very few black women who were interned by the Germans in the Besançon POW camp in occupied France. Nothing more is known about her.

Two other black POWs, Cy Grant and Johnny Smythe, were interviewed in various journals and left detailed testimonies about their experiences.[2] In 1939 in British Guiana, Cy Grant's father wanted him to go into the ministry, but Cy knew he had no specific calling for it:

> … though I thought at one stage that I'd go into it because it would give me an opportunity to get a university education. But then the Second World War came and I applied for aircrew in the Royal Air Force.[3]

When the policy towards recruiting black men was changed, Cy was one of the first men from the colonies to join the RAF. Cy was posted to 103 Squadron, based at RAF Elsham Wolds in Lincolnshire. He was a member of a mixed Canadian and British seven-man crew of a Lancaster bomber. He qualified as navigator and astronomical navigator on 5 February 1943. He later said, although it was almost impossible for a black recruit to be a pilot he never experienced any racism in the RAF.

Cy flew on bombing missions over the Ruhr and in June 1943 he was shot down over Holland on his third mission during the massive offensive over Germany:

> We dived steeply in an effort to smother the flames, but when we levelled out the flames had spread. Then one of the wheels of the undercarriage fell away in a flaming circle. Now we were up against it. By the time we reached the coast, we

were a flaming comet over the Dutch sky. Both wings were on fire now and I gave the shortest course to the English coast. Unfortunately we were flying into a headwind of about 80 miles an hour at 20,000 feet. Undaunted, we had unanimously decided to risk getting across the Channel rather than turn back and bail out over occupied territory. But it was becoming extremely difficult for Al to control the aircraft and he sensed that we would not make it across the Channel. He decided to turn back over land.[4]

Al, the pilot, was forced to make a decision that would change Cy's life. With no other options available, he ordered his crew to bail out. Cy recalled that dramatic moment. He landed in a field south of Nieuw-Vennep and hid in a cornfield for most of the day, but two of the crew of had been killed outright, including the Canadian tail gunner.

Cy was aware that Germans were searching for survivors of the crash. He had been instructed to escape to Spain but he realised that, as a black man in occupied Europe, it would be impossible for him to undertake this task without attracting attention. His only hope was to seek help from the Dutch. In the early evening he managed to attract the attention of a farmer who took him to his farm, where his wife tended to a small cut on his head and fed him. However, a local Dutch policeman had heard he was there and, after collecting Cy, handed him over to the Germans.

Cy was taken to an interrogation camp in Amsterdam and placed in solitary confinement for five days. A few days later he was transported with many other POWs to the camp known as Stalag Luft III (later the scene of *The Great Escape*), before being sent to another POW camp a few kilometres away. He later said, 'For the most part my captivity was painless. At least we were alive.'[5] There were no other black officers in the POW camp and Cy found that there was no obvious racism directed towards him.

Cy's artistic talent proved useful in the POW camp:

The fellows used to bring me photographs of their girlfriends and I made portraits, enlargements, from these photographs, for a bar of chocolate or three packs of cigarettes. So we kept ourselves occupied. Everyone wanted to try and escape, and everyone was roped in, even just to keep an eye on the guards. There was always activity.[6]

As a POW, Cy discovered that he had a great deal of time to reflect on the direction of his life and what he wanted to do after he got out:

I met a lot of good people because, as an officer in the RAF, you were among the cream of officers. I met all sorts of people, including writers, schoolteachers, lecturers and scientists. And, living for two years close together, I learnt a great deal and asked a lot of questions – that's where I matured, actually. I decided then, that I would study law, because I wanted to go back to the Caribbean. My ambition was to help get the British out of the West Indies.[7]

Cy described the worst part of his imprisonment as occurring during the last few months of the war. The officers' POW camp where Cy had been imprisoned for two years was evacuated with the approach of the Soviet Army in early 1945, 'Forced marches in deep snow for days on end with little rations, sleeping in barns, then transported in cattle trucks jammed together like sardines in a tin.'[8]

After days of trudging through snow, the prisoners found themselves in a lice-ridden POW camp at Luckenwalde, about 50km south of Berlin. As the war raged on and the Soviet Army came closer, the German guards began to vacate their posts, 'We were freed by the advancing Russian army who tore down part of the perimeter fence with their tanks'.

Cy returned to England and stayed in the RAF for another year or so. Around this time, a special section of the Colonial Office was set up to offer assistance to black airmen:

They were having a lot of hassles as you can imagine, and they needed people to defend them at court martials and other disputes. So that was my job for about a year, which also fitted in with my plans. When I was finally demobbed, I went to study law at Middle Temple and was called to the Bar in 1950.[9]

John 'Johnny' Smythe was born into a middle-class family in Freetown, Sierra Leone, West Africa. At school his teacher gave him a copy of Adolf Hitler's book *Mein Kampf*:

I read what this man was going to do to the blacks if he gets into power. He vowed to use the heart of black people to make shoe soles. And he attacked the British and Americans for encouraging the blacks to become doctors and lawyers. It was a book which would put any black man's back up and it put mine up. I grew up with hate for this man and his cronies and was pleased when I had the opportunity to fight against him.[10]

When war came in 1939, Johnny served with the Sierra Leone Defence Corps before volunteering to serve his king and country in the RAF. In 1940 he travelled from his home in Freetown to the Scottish town of Greenock where he undertook training. In 1941, Johnny went on his first mission:

We knew what lay ahead of us. Every day we counted the number that returned. We also knew that there was a good chance that we would not return. We met with our first serious trouble during an operation over Mainz in Germany. The plane had several times been pelted by flak and it was in a bad state. Although we lost one of our engines, we still managed to limp back home.[11]

After nearly eighteen months of working as a navigator, Johnny, who had first become a sergeant, found himself promoted to flying officer. He was one of only four who were selected out of ninety, and this made him immensely proud:

> Standing in front of the noticeboard, I still refused to believe what I saw and read. An officer of the RAF! From that moment my life was completely changed. I no longer ate with the other ranks and I socialised only in the officers' mess. In effect, I was no longer one of the boys, although I often went to town with some of the airmen for a beer. Airmen had to salute me all the time. What made me so uncomfortable as an officer was not that I was the only black man to be promoted to that rank, but I was the only black man in the entire camp. [12]

Johnny acknowledged that the selection of his crew was extremely important, because they had to work as a team. 'We were brothers in trouble, comrades in arms, and we needed to stick together and understand each other. We were posted to a squadron of the new Lancaster bombers; a plane superior to the Stirling.' [13] The crew's first mission was uneventful, but they dreaded their second:

> Before setting out, I had my Bible in my jacket pocket and butterflies in my stomach. Every day we counted the number of planes that returned, and the thought of not returning to base haunted us. We went – and returned unscathed. During these first few weeks of operations, we averaged about three bombing missions per week.

On his twenty-seventh mission, on the night of 18 November 1943, Johnny's luck ran out. He was the navigator aboard a Short Stirling III heavy bomber of 623 Squadron, one of 395 aircraft dispatched to attack the German city of Mannheim. The aircraft was crippled by anti-aircraft fire, and the crew was forced to parachute from the stricken aircraft:

We were flying at 16,000 feet when the fighters came out of nowhere. They raked the fuselage and there were flames everywhere. Then the searchlights caught us. I was hit by shrapnel. Pieces came from underneath, piercing my abdomen, going through my side. Another came through my seat and into my groin. I heard the pilot ordering us to bail out. The pilot made it, but three of the seven-man crew were not so fortunate and we lost them. We jumped out and up to that point I never realised how seriously injured I was, because I did not feel any pain. We all parachuted and I landed among some trees. We had some rough ones before but this seemed to be the end. I have tried to forget that night.

Johnny hid in a barn, but German soldiers opened fire, spraying it with bullets. Johnny surrendered but when they saw him the Germans couldn't believe their eyes. They were shocked to see a black man who was also an officer. They could not reconcile this with the Nazi propaganda with which they had been indoctrinated: that the black man was subhuman. Johnny said they just stood there gazing.

After spending one week in hospital, receiving treatment for his injuries, Johnny was taken to Frankfurt for interrogation. This was his first encounter with the SS or 'Swastika boys', as he referred to them:

> They saw me like a prized possession … The spectacle of a black officer in the RAF was just not real. Some probably believed that this was another example of the English sense of humour in its most grotesque form.[14]

When his interrogators realised that Johnny was not going to offer them information, he was reunited with his pilot and rear gunner and sent to a POW camp.

For the next eighteen months they were prisoners of the Nazis in Stalag Luft I, a camp for 9,000 Allied airmen in Barth, a small

German town on the Baltic Sea. Stalag I had opened as a camp for British officers in 1942. American airmen began to arrive early in 1943. On his arrival, some trigger-happy German guards murdered several prisoners in front of Johnny:

> One day we found out that the Germans had taken away all the Jewish prisoners. There was talk of an incinerator being built just outside the camp in anticipation of a German victory. The effect on us was paralysing and demoralising.[15]

At the camp, Johnny continued to shock the Germans. Prison guards were dumbstruck when they saw him in an RAF officer's uniform, but they did not treat him differently from the white prisoners.

Johnny kept himself busy in the camp and enthusiastically joined the escape committee. He helped other prisoners to escape, but he couldn't break out himself. 'I don't think a six-foot-five black man would've got very far,' he said.

Then one day in May 1945, 'we woke up and, to our utter amazement and disbelief, there was not a single German guard in sight. They had all abandoned their posts and fled.' A few days later, when the camp was liberated by the Soviet Army, one of their officers embraced Johnny and gave him vodka.

16

Lilian and Ramsay Bader

When Lilian Bailey lost her job with the NAAFI due to the colour bar (see Chapter 2), she returned to domestic service. But she remained determined to join up. In 1940 she heard a group of West Indians on the radio. They told the interviewer they had been rejected by the army but recruited into the RAF.

Lilian decided to try for a position in the air force and was thrilled when, on 28 March 1941 (almost one and a half years after being discharged from the NAAFI), she was recruited by the Women's Auxiliary Air Force (WAAF). She found herself 'the only coloured person in this sea of white faces'.[1] After qualifying as an Instrument Repairer II, in December 1941 Lilian became a leading aircraftwoman (LACW) and soon gained the rank of acting corporal.

With the newly acquired corporal's stripes, Lilian sat at the dining table reserved for junior NCOs (non-commissioned officers). To her, this was an achievement to be proud of. 'I couldn't wait to go and get my stripes and stitch them on. But I felt I had achieved something which, although it seems small now, was a lot to me then.'[2]

Through her former landlady in Yorkshire, Lilian made contact with a young British-born mixed-race soldier called Ramsay Bader. He was a tank driver who was serving with the 147th (Essex Yeomanry) Field Regiment Royal Artillery. He was the son of a soldier from Freetown, Sierra Leone, and an English mother, but he had been adopted at the age of six months and raised by a white family in Essex. His adopted father was Ernst Bader, a German-Swiss businessman who had become a naturalised Englishman. Ramsay took his adopted father's surname.

Lilian and Ramsay exchanged letters and photographs. Until then, Lilian had rarely encountered other black people, especially in the forces, and Lilian immediately felt attracted to Ramsay:

> Even in the ugly khaki battle dress, he looked like an officer. We both had religious backgrounds; his was Methodist though his parents had become Quakers. His voice was low, practically without an accent, and he did not swear or say anything which would destroy the respectable image I had formed. It was a relief to meet a coloured boy-friend for a change. I had met no other coloured WAAFs, and only seen an Indian RAF officer and one coloured airman who appeared fleetingly at Condover.[3]

Lilian and Ramsay were married in 1943 in Hull:

> We had a quiet little wedding: no music and no flowers on the altar. My wedding cake had a plaster of Paris top which when removed showed a chocolate or ginger cake! We spent the night at a hotel and Hitler duly celebrated with an air raid.[4]

Lilian's chances of further promotion in the WAAF were curtailed when she discovered she was expecting a baby. She received her discharge in February 1944.

When Ramsay left school at the age of 16, in spite of having achieved good qualifications, he faced difficulty finding a job because of his colour, 'So my adopted father sent me to Stratford to work in one of his factories. I stayed there until I got my calling up papers for the army in 1939.'[5] Ramsay said that when the war broke out, he was aware of Hitler's attitude to black people because he remembered Hitler's appalling treatment of the African American athlete Jesse Owens at the 1936 Olympics in Berlin:

> Why should human beings be treated like that when the Olympics is for sport for every nationality? I couldn't understand it and it made me want to fight against this sort of thing because having read what Hitler was doing to the Jews, the coloured would be next for the gas chamber. I was born in Britain and accepted it as my country and I must fight for what I believe in, which I still think today. I did the right thing. During the war there was a friendly attitude from most service people and I didn't feel too much prejudice because we were all fighting for the same cause. My brother was a sergeant major, decorated, and we served with all the other people who fought for the survival of mankind.[6]

On 6 June 1944, Ramsay was one of thousands of soldiers engaged in the D-Day landings:

> We felt very sick, having not experienced this type of heavy swell which you get in the Channel, and the terrible loss of life, seeing floating bodies who had been hit by shells that had come in from the enemy. Although resistance from the enemy wasn't supposed to be very strong we still met quite strong pockets of resistance.[7]

Ramsay discovered the French people they were helping to liberate were not always very friendly towards the British soldiers:

> … because they remembered Dunkirk in 1940, and they were not sure if we were going to be pushed back into the sea again.

German sniping was always there. But the Free French and the resistance always helped us. Finally we made for the town of Bayeux. With the Americans on our right and the Canadians further down all these helped to form a bridgehead which was finally held.[8]

It was an anxious time for Lilian, and she prayed that her husband would survive:

For long periods you wouldn't get any news at all from the second front, the Normandy landings, because the mail didn't get through. At one stage I didn't know if Ramsay was alive or dead but you just kept going and I remember kneeling in the chapel and praying like blazes that Ramsay would be saved. It was a terrible time because you knew some people were going to be killed, and Ramsay couldn't swim! He hated water. That's what worried me more than anything, but he came through.[9]

Interviewed for the Imperial War Museum in 1989, Ramsay explained that, after the Second World War, he found out that he had an older brother called Benjamin MacRae. He had also served in the British Army. 'We met up. He had served in Burma during the war, but our mother had died, so I never met her. I learned that our Sierra Leonean father had served in the First World War.'[10]

Benjamin joined the army in January 1940. He later recalled for the Imperial War Museum the feeling of comradeship he experienced at the start of the war:

All chaps of my own age. It was a little bit of an adventure. Nobody really knew what was happening. Training was a bit of a mixture. Laughable. Sad. We all got on well. We was young and there was always an element of adventure to it.[11]

Benjamin was sent to India for training. He took part in the Burma Campaign against the Japanese and was awarded the Military Medal for his services.

Ramsay died in 1992 at the age of 73. Benjamin died in 2001 at the age of 83. In 2008, at the age of 90, Lilian attended the opening of the Imperial War Museum's 'From War to Windrush' exhibition. She died in 2015 at the age of 97.

17

Auxiliary Territorial Service

Briefly the Army Council consider that it would be wrong to encourage coloured women to come from the West Indies at their own expense as they would be unused to the climatic conditions and modes of life in England and, in fact, some of them we might not be able to accept. The Council feel, therefore, that any demand by the West Indian women to be enrolled in a uniformed service would be better met by a local organisation.

> Letter from the War Office to the Colonial Office,
> London, 8 December 1941

Despite resistance from the War Office, black West Indian women were recruited for the services, but not without a struggle and not until 1943, four years into the war. However, it is impossible to know exactly how many of them came to Britain to join the Women's Auxiliary Air Force (WAAF) and the Auxiliary Territorial Service (ATS), the women's branch of the British Army in wartime.

Different sources give conflicting figures. In May 1943, when the War Office told the Colonial Office that they would only accept 'suitable European women from the Colonies into the ATS', it was declared that around twenty black women were already serving with the ATS. However, it was believed that these women had all been living in Britain before they joined up and had not travelled from the Caribbean. One of them was the British-born Norma Quaye, who joined the ATS in 1939. There were also a handful of black women in the WAAF, including Liverpool-born Lilian Bailey, who had joined in 1941 (see Chapter 16).

One who almost didn't make it was Miss L. Curtis from Bermuda. In October 1941 she applied to join the ATS and was provisionally accepted by the War Office. When it was discovered that she was black, Miss Curtis was informed that there was no suitable vacancy. Historian Joanne Buggins said:

> The Governor of Bermuda warned that this rejection would have a most demoralising effect locally, and the Colonial Office was adamant that whatever might happen on the general issue it was quite indefensible that the Department should go back on a definite commitment to Miss Curtis … Only when the Secretary of State for the Colonies, Colonel Oliver Stanley, intervened was this matter settled.[1]

However, it took time for the matter to be settled. In 1943, as the war intensified, this particular 'colour bar' finally ended and black West Indian women were invited to join the ATS. The response to the call for recruits was immediate and some women were so keen to 'join up' that they were prepared to pay for their passage to Britain. The women who were recruited to the ATS began to arrive in Britain in October 1943 and the first group included Miss L. Curtis.

Most sources claim that, in October 1943, thirty black women from across the Caribbean were the first to arrive in Britain. However, Ben Bousquet has stated:

> 381 women actually paid their way across to fight for King and country. They were nice middle-class black women who

wouldn't have done anything anyway other than stay at home. So, the war was a form of elevation, a release.[2]

In British Honduras (now Belize), Nadia Cattouse was one of the first women from the Caribbean to respond to the recruitment drive to join the ATS. 'They asked for volunteers. I heard this on the local radio news and I was so eager I jumped on my bike straight away to get to Drill Hall.'[3] In June 1944, at the age of 19, she arrived in London via Scotland:

> There were only six of us when I journeyed overseas, and we arrived on a ship packed with thousands of American soldiers. I had no contact with American southerners. I was lucky! When our train arrived in London an air-raid siren went, and I was surprised that everyone strolled around so calm. I couldn't understand this. Then we were directed to an underground shelter. So, my first impression of London is the air-raid siren! I can't remember how long we stayed in London but shortly after our arrival we were sent to the ATS headquarters in Guildford in Surrey for basic training.[4]

Nadia turned down the opportunity to become a drill sergeant:

> I was the only one who volunteered for the Royal Signals Corps in Edinburgh where I trained as a signals operator. In Edinburgh there was no racial tension. No problem at all. We had camaraderie. I just knew I was heading for Scotland. I think it was because the colony and the settlement of British Honduras were peopled by Scottish-British far more than by the English-British, especially in the early days. Also, the British Honduran Forestry Unit were already in place in Scotland and I had an uncle, Carlton Fairweather, among them.[5]

In 1944 Norma Best joined the ATS in British Honduras. When she was interviewed by a group of students from the

Alexander Park Secondary School in Haringey for Patrick Vernon's documentary, *Speaking Out and Standing Firm* (2010), Norma explained:

> I volunteered because I wanted to travel and we didn't have many opportunities to travel in those days. And that was the only opportunity so I thought I was going to have it. So I applied and I was accepted.

When the teenagers enquired about her army service and racism, Norma replied:

> Serving in the armed forces was wonderful. It was the best experience I've ever had. We were treated well. Our officers looked after us like our mothers. Every step I made in the army was fantastic. I didn't experience any racism because at that time all the people in England wanted to win the war, so colour didn't come into it. We were all fighting for the same thing, to win the war. The English people opened their homes to us, we were invited out for dinners, teas, no problems at all. There were problems with the American forces, but it didn't hinder us.

The war changed Norma's life and enabled her to fulfil her dreams, 'I was looking for adventure. A few of my relatives and friends said that London was cold and that I might not be able to withstand the weather, but I was determined to go.'[6]

Norma left home and arrived in Scotland in August 1944. She took a train to London where she was allowed to do some sightseeing before going to Guildford for six weeks of training. On her arrival, she discovered that she knew more about Britain than some of the British. She put that down to her *very* English education. She was also surprised by the accents. 'I thought everyone would speak proper English! I was stunned when I heard the Scottish accent, or the Cockney accent.'[7]

In 2010, she told the students from Alexander Park Secondary School:

> The training was tough but we did it. We used to get up to mischief. Sometimes we used to take it in turns to hide, not go on parade, because we used to wear shorts for sports in the snow. But it was all done with love.

Norma's ambition was to be a driver but she could not cope with the weather. Instead, she undertook administrative work, serving in Preston and later Derby. Norma remembered her time serving in the ATS:

> You had to be in at certain times. You had to do certain jobs at certain times and when you went out you had to be on your best behaviour because you're wearing that uniform and whatever you do will reflect on others. The training I received strengthened me in character. But what was in me remained there.[8]

After war was declared in 1939, Connie Mark remembered 'a mood of fear in Jamaica'. She said the English 'put the fear of God in us':

> We were definitely positively told that the Germans wanted us because we were a stepping stone to the coast of America. So we were on our tenterhooks all the time. Like England, Jamaica is an island. We depended on boats bringing things in. So if you are short of oil because the boat coming in was torpedoed, then the whole bloody island has no oil.[9]

Connie also remembered the English officers who would:

> … go into all the little corners of Jamaica and they would beg, literally beg you to come and fight for England because

we were brought up that England was our mother country and obviously when your mother has problems, you've got to come and help her.[10]

Connie was made aware of the dangers that surrounded Jamaica and the other islands of the Caribbean. Ships were vulnerable to being torpedoed by the German U-boats. 'Guyana had a lot of gold and the Germans wanted to get it, and they also wanted oil from Trinidad, so there was a lot of submarines watching the island. It was very frightening.'[11] Connie remembered the air-raid wardens who went around the towns and villages in Jamaica, 'If by chance you had a speck of light showing from your house, you'd be arrested and fined.'[12]

Connie was born Kingston, Jamaica, and saw herself as British, and patriotic, 'England was our mother country. We were brought up to respect the Royal Family. I used to collect pictures of Princess Margaret and Princess Elizabeth. I adored them.'[13]

Connie was just 19 years old in 1943 when she joined the ATS in Jamaica. Unlike other women from the Caribbean islands who joined up, Connie served in the ATS in Jamaica for ten years. She worked as a medical secretary at the British Military Hospital in Kingston. Her duties included typing up the medical reports of those who had been injured in battle. Connie found herself documenting the terrible injuries men had sustained in bombings and combat:

When you are in the army you are on 24 hours duty. You know nothing about off duty, so I used to have my uniform hung up all the while. I lived with my aunt and anywhere I was going my aunt had to know where I was because if a troop ship was coming in at 2 a.m. in the morning then the Military Police would come to my home, knock on the door and, in five minutes flat, I had to be dressed to go out. If I wasn't there my aunt would have to say she's gone to a night club here and there. The Military Police would come to get me wherever I was and I had to be down at that troop ship. And that's really when the reality of war came home to me because you saw men leaving hale and hearty and you see them coming back on stretchers, you see them coming back in wheelchairs, some blind.[14]

Connie remembered the fights that broke out, especially when the Irish Fusiliers arrived in Jamaica:

They all got drunk and they used to fight! They fought the Jamaicans they met in bars. And of course when they're coming to go to camp the Jamaicans waylaid them. So sometimes a whole road had to be put out of bounds because of fighting white soldiers. And we had the Brockville Rifles from Canada. And they could fight! They were always fighting! But a lot of it was prejudices, you see. They are white and they come to Jamaica and they just couldn't handle it. They just felt that they was kings, that, 'I can do anything and go anywhere.' And of course Jamaican soldiers – no, not necessarily soldiers but Jamaicans whether soldiers or not – took exceptions to it. So they started some nice good fight. Fortunately with the Americans it wasn't so bad because the Americans wasn't in Kingston. They were in St Catherine, in another parish. Their base was actually in a place called Sandy Gully. We did not have that much to do with them. But everyone wanted to go and work on the American base because the pay was good.[15]

Eventually Connie rose to the rank of corporal:

It was quite an achievement to even reach the rank of Corporal. When you are a Lance Corporal, army regulations state that once one is promoted to Corporal you are entitled to tuppence per day. I applied for my tuppence a day and was turned down by the War Office. When I asked why, I was told the Jamaican ATS were not entitled to this. I was in a British regiment attached to the Royal Army Medical Corps but I was still not entitled. That was my first experience of racial discrimination. The Queen still owes me eight years of tuppence a day! That may not sound a lot now, but in those days it added up. So I have had my little prejudices thrown at me.[16]

When the war ended, Connie's commander put her up for the British Empire Medal (BEM), but she did not receive it. She believed she was overlooked because she refused to clean the houses of the English ATS officers. However, in 1992, she did finally receive the BEM, nearly forty years after she had left Jamaica and made London her home.

18

'They'll Bleed and Suffer and Die': African American GIs in Britain

Joe Louis, the world-famous professional boxer, served in the US Army during the Second World War. While on a morale-boosting tour of Britain in 1944, he objected to the racial segregation the US Army tried to force on the British people. He said:

> This wasn't America, this was England. The theatre manager knew who I was and apologized. Said he had instructions from the Army … they had no business messing up another country's customs with American Jim Crow.[1]

In May 1942, shortly after America had entered the war on 7 December 1941, American GIs began to arrive in Britain. During the Second World War, around 3 million American service personnel came to Britain. Among them were 130,000 African Americans who were segregated and subjected to an appalling degree of discrimination. By 12 May 1942 there were only 811 African American GIs in Britain, but by the end of 1942 the figure had risen to 7,315.

Until 1942, the majority of white Britons had not come into contact with black people, but during the war most of them encountered the African American GIs, or at least heard about them. The British public was also confronted with America's racial segregation policies and racist attitudes, especially those held by citizens of the southern states. Unlike their British comrades, American troops were racially segregated, and remained that way until 1948 when a presidential order from Harry S. Truman put an end to it.

When African American men began to enlist in the army in 1940, they were trained almost entirely for non-combatant roles, such as labourers, transport operators, stevedores, kitchen and domestic staff and stewards. They were not permitted to enlist in the Army Air Corps or in the Marine Corps. In Britain, the practice of racial segregation continued after the American armed forces arrived. Black and white troops were to be kept separate, but 'equal', at work and while they were off duty.

On their arrival in Britain in 1942, white American troops were cautioned about making racist comments in the presence of the British public, and they had to be informed that racial segregation on the scale they had in the USA did not exist in Britain. A colour bar existed in some public places, but Britain did not racially segregate on transport, or in restaurants, as they did throughout the southern states and in some of the northern states of the USA.

In *'Over Here': The GIs in Wartime Britain*, Juliet Gardiner said that officially the British Government distanced itself from the American army's policy of racial segregation:

But if there was no official support for the US measures of segregation, there were many in government and local administration who were anxious to place strict limits on contacts between the black US troops and the British population, particularly the female population. In August 1942, a conference at the War Office in London agreed that British officers should explain American racial attitudes so that their own troops, especially those women who were members of the ATS, might avoid contact with black GIs … The British government was balancing on a knife edge – covertly supporting US Army segregation while overtly declining to assist in implementing it.[2]

Many British people were upset with the appalling treatment of African American GIs who, in their opinion, had come to help in the fight against Hitler and Nazism. An unidentified Cambridge man expressed his disgust:

> I think the treatment of the coloured races of the US Army etc by the white fellows is disgusting. The coloured are prohibited from going to certain pubs, dancing halls, cinemas, just because the white fellows are snobbish. After all, both races are doing the same job of work.[3]

An unnamed Birmingham man also expressed his shock at the racism he witnessed on the streets of his city, 'I have personally seen the American troops kick, and I mean, kick coloured soldiers off the pavements, and when asked why, reply "stinking black pigs" or "black trash" or "uppity n★★★★★★".'[4]

The white GIs did not restrict their violence to their black countrymen. In 1943, a West Indian airman sat with his (white) comrades in a canteen for Allied troops when an American airman walked in:

> [And] seeing the coloured airman quietly sitting at a table, strolled up to him and slashed [slapped] him across the face! Of course everyone jumped up ready for a fight but the proprietress managed to stop it. Someone said 'send for the U.S. police' but the Americans tried to pass it off, and said that if the coloured man would go, everything would be all right. The British said if anyone ought to go it was the American. A schoolmistress who was helping at the back, dashed out and slashed [slapped] the American's face, and her language was

very choice! Anyway, they smuggled him out, but our men said if they saw him again they'd kill him … Meanwhile the coloured man sat there as if dazed, it was unexpected and so unwarranted. It seems amazing that the Americans are fighting on our side, when you hear things like that.[5]

At a Cabinet meeting in October 1942, Lord Salisbury, Secretary of State for the Colonies, spoke of the increasing difficulties and informed everyone about a black civil servant from the Colonial Office who had recently been refused a table at a restaurant he regularly frequented because American officers had complained about his presence. Philip Ziegler's *London at War 1939–1945* gave Winston Churchill's response: 'That's all right,' commented the prime minister, 'if he takes a banjo with him they'll think he's one of the band!'[6]

In many instances, when 'official' support or protection was absent, individuals took their own stand against the Americans. Jack Artis, a black British Army sergeant, born in Worcester, loathed the white American GIs, 'We were there to fight the Nazis, who believed in white supremacy, so God alone knows what they [the GIs] thought they were fighting for'.[7]

However, some white Britons might just as well have come from Alabama or Mississippi. On 6 September 1942, the *Sunday Pictorial* published an article with the headline, 'Vicar's Wife Insults Our Allies'. In Worle, near Weston-super-Mare, the Vicar's wife, Mrs May, presented local women with a 'six-point code' which she advised them to follow if any African American GIs came to their village. These (in her own words) were the rules Mrs May laid down:

1. If a local woman keeps a shop and a coloured soldier enters, she must serve him, but she must do it as quickly as possible and indicate that she does not desire him to come there again.
2. If she is in a cinema and notices a coloured soldier next to her, she moves to another seat immediately.

3. If she is walking on the pavement and a coloured soldier is coming towards her, she crosses to the other pavement.

4. If she is in a shop and a coloured soldier enters, she leaves as soon as she has made her purchase or before that if she is in a queue.

5. White women, of course, must have no social relationship with coloured troops.

6. On no account must coloured troops be invited to the homes of white women.

To their credit, the women of the village were angered by this, and refused to adopt the code, which they found insulting. A local woman told the *Sunday Pictorial*, 'I was disgusted, and so were most of the women. We have no intention of agreeing to her decree.' The *Sunday Pictorial* made the following assurance to the black GIs:

Any coloured soldier who reads this may rest assured that there is no colour bar in this country and that he is as welcome as any other Allied soldier. He will find that the vast majority of people have nothing but repugnance for the narrow-minded uninformed prejudices expressed by the vicar's wife. There is – and will be – no persecution of coloured people in Britain.

The persecution of black GIs by some of their white compatriots began to escalate as the numbers of black GIs coming to serve in Britain increased. There were many confrontations, but censorship forbade any reporting of them in the British press.

One of the worst incidents occurred on 23–24 June 1943 at Bamber Bridge near Preston, Lancashire. A group of African American soldiers had been relaxing in Ye Old Hobb Inn, the public house in the village of Bamber, when a confrontation between them and some white military police began. Villagers had welcomed the black soldiers, and they were appalled by the racist attitudes of the military police. The incident then escalated into a full-scale battle and there was shooting on both sides. One black soldier, Private William Crossland, was killed. Two black soldiers and a white officer were wounded.

The incident became known as 'The Battle of Bamber Bridge' and the investigation that followed placed much of the blame on the military police and the white officers who joined in the fight. Consequently, the ranks of this command were purged of inexperienced and racist officers, and the military police patrols were racially integrated. The morale of African American troops stationed in Britain, which was at risk of hitting an all-time low, improved over time. There were, however, several more minor conflicts between black and white American troops in Britain during the rest of the war.

Baron Baker, a Jamaican who joined the RAF in 1944, recalled that the first major racial problem he experienced occurred with the American soldiers. In a pub in Gloucester he and his friends were told by American GIs that 'back home, n★★★★★★ aren't allowed in our bars'. There hadn't been any problems at this pub before the Americans arrived. He said:

> There was a vast difference between black English service-men to the American black because in the southern states of America if you're black you stay in the back. Some people call it racism. Some people call it apartheid. But to me that is naked, stinking, downright Hitler's fascism. That was something unac-ceptable to us Jamaicans. The American white servicemen who think they could take over Gloucester, we had news for them, because when they set upon us, we retaliate, and we retaliate in such a way that one night they had to use British laddies with sten guns to pick us up in town, put us on a lorry, and take us back to camp.[8]

Following this incident, the proud, defiant and outspoken Baker confronted both his group captain and the American commander when he feared that Jamaican soldiers would be barred from socialising with whites. He informed them:

> We are King George VI's soldiers, *not* Roosevelt's little black boys. We are not foreigners. We are British subjects and this is the mother country and you as a Yankee foreigner ain't beating us one inch from where we are.

By D-Day, 6 June 1944, it was estimated that there were there were around 130,000 black GIs based in Britain. In July 1944, after a number of minor clashes, a major confrontation between over 400 black soldiers and military police in Bristol city centre 'exploded' into a full-scale riot. Professor Neil A. Wynn recounted:

> Although the Bristol *Evening Post* dismissed the event as a mere 'Local Fracas', and made no mention of its racial dimension, the streets had to be closed off with buses, and 120 military policemen were used to quell the unrest. One African American was killed and dozens were wounded. According to some reports a number of local people had encouraged the African Americans during the fighting: elsewhere they were said to have joined in against white Americans. As one reporter to the British American Liaison Board noted, 'It was probably quite true that the British people sided with the Negroes simply because they always side with those they consider to be the underdogs'.[9]

One of the main causes of tensions was the mixing of black GIs with white women. Professor Wynn said, 'In the view of some British people, African Americans, like the rest of their countrymen, were not just "Over Paid, Over Fed", but also "Over Sexed and Over Here".'

In *Rich Relations: The American Occupation of Britain, 1942–1945*, David Reynolds notes that official reports showed that the

British public disapproved of racial mixing, and quotes the strong reaction of novelist Ann Meader:

> In the hothouse atmosphere of Weston-super-Mare in October 1942, [she] was appalled to see two black GIs with two fair-haired white girls. She felt for a moment that the girls should be 'shot' for risking 'coloured blood' in their children.[10]

Professor Wynn commented:

> Inevitably, some illegitimate children resulted from these wartime sexual encounters and they became known as 'Brown Babies'. Estimates of the number of such children born to black and white couples range from 500 to 2,000 ... The fate of most of these children is uncertain: some were placed in orphanages while others were brought up by their mothers or relatives.[11]

In Liverpool, Pastor Daniels Ekarte, who had come to Britain from Nigeria, was a well-known and highly respected minister and community leader. He became involved in the welfare of the 'Brown Babies'. The American army would not give permission for the black GIs to marry the white mothers, so Ekarte lobbied the government for action on the children's behalf. He even gave shelter to some of them at his African Churches Mission in Toxteth.

With help and support from the fundraising efforts of Learie Constantine, Ekarte tried to purchase a larger property to use as a children's home, but the government did nothing to support him and Ekarte failed to raise the money needed for the home. In a dawn raid, the eight children at the mission were dragged away and dispersed around the country by Liverpool Social Services.

In 1945, the American army finally permitted black members of the Women's Army Corps (WAC) to serve overseas. They were an all-black unit called the 6888th Central Postal Directory Battalion. Based in Birmingham, and later in France, their job was to route mail to millions of service personnel based in Europe; much of it had been piling up in English warehouses. The commander of the unit was Major Charity Adams, the first African American to be commissioned an officer in the WAC (in August 1942) and one of only two black women to hold a wartime rank in the WAC as high as major.

When the 6888th postal unit arrived in Birmingham, incorporating over 700 women, they were the first black women many white people in the city had ever seen. They were given a rousing welcome when they arrived. Crowds of locals came out to watch as the parade of uniformed black women passed by.

To summarise, most African American servicemen and women were given a warm welcome by the British people. Professor Phillip McGuire said:

> It was generally considered – by British public opinion and by American travellers and journalists – that most British people accepted black soldiers as American soldiers without regard to race and color; however, the problem lay in the importation of American racial patterns to Britain by American white troops, resulting in clashes, ideological and physical, between American soldiers. Thus black troops felt that, instead of leaving problems of this sort at home, the [white] Americans tried to instil their ways and actions over here.[12]

Although white Americans tried to instil their ways and actions, it is to the credit of the British people that the majority of them resisted. Juliet Gardiner, in *Wartime: Britain 1939–1945*, recounted the memories of Mary Kemp, who was at a dance in her home town in Somerset when a group of black GIs arrived:

> Nobody talked to them. We thought it was very rude so we decided to ask the band to play a Palais Glide and make it

a 'ladies' choice', and my sister and I and some friends went over to ask them to dance, which they did. And that broke the ice. But afterwards someone came up to my father and asked him what his daughters were doing dancing with coloured troops. My father replied that he was proud of us. 'They're our allies too,' he said. 'They'll bleed and suffer and die, just like the white men.'[13]

19

'A Shameful Business': The Case of George Roberts

In 1944 the *Guardian* newspaper and the *News Letter* of the LCP reported on an incident involving George Roberts, a West Indian electrician who had volunteered to come to Britain to support the war effort. His journey had taken him from his home in Antigua in the Caribbean to Liverpool in December 1942 where he took a job in a munitions factory.

Roberts had joined as a volunteer, without compulsion, and he carried out his duties without incident until October 1943 when he was reported for failing to attend his Home Guard duties without reasonable excuse. He explained that he failed to attend because he had been refused admission to a dance hall on account of his colour. He had returned to the dance hall wearing his Home Guard uniform, but had again been refused. Police at the entrance did not stop him, but when he asked for a ticket he was told, 'Sorry we cannot sell you a ticket because you are a coloured man'. On this particular night there were a lot of African American GIs about and the American military police were keeping them away from the dance hall.

Roberts was prosecuted for the offence of refusing to undertake his Home Guard duties, and a fine of £5 was imposed. An appeal against the verdict was made, which was not heard until the quarter session of August 1944. Learie Constantine gave evidence on behalf of Roberts. He described him as a 'very good character'. Roberts was represented by Rose Heilbron. Her outstanding career as a defence barrister included many 'firsts' for a woman. For example, she became the first woman judge to sit at the Old Bailey.

Mr Edward Hemmerde KC, the Liverpool Recorder and a former Liberal MP, denounced the 'colour bar' that Roberts had experienced. He was:

> … clearly outraged at Roberts' predicament, especially since technically he had broken the law and thus had to be fined. The Recorder like many others felt that during the current period of strife things should be different in Liverpool. There should be no discrimination, especially towards those who were aiding the war effort.[1]

Hemmerde reduced the fine of £5 imposed on Roberts to just one farthing. He commented:

> If anything that I may say may offend citizens of some other Allied countries, let me say that the Allied nations make up the democratic world, and if they have a colour prejudice they must occasionally come into collision with people who have not. I happen to be one who has not.

Giving judgement, he said:

> I do not understand how in the British Empire, with so many coloured people as its citizens, anything in the way of a colour bar can exist or ever be allowed to exist by any Government that is worth the name of Government. When people come here to risk their lives they are entitled to think that they are coming to conditions of decency and order in a country that

claims the title of imperial in its best sense. If they find that a noisy and intolerant minority are not prepared to give them equal rights, I think they have a right to be angry. I think it is impertinence for any country to accept the aid of coloured people from any part of the world and then to say: 'Our laws don't enable us to deal with you on terms of complete equality' ... If you accept aid from coloured people you accept them, as your friends and as people whose aid you are proud to receive, and they should be the first to receive justice at your hands. But they do not receive it, and it is a shameful business. Mr. Roberts is breaking the law, when, having come here to serve the country, he refuses to be insulted. The fact that he is guilty may be more the object of laughter than anything else ... We would like to remind all dance hall proprietors that discrimination against Negroes is exactly the same kidney as Nazi discrimination against Jews. It is a very dangerous policy for them to pursue in Britain, law or no law.[2]

In August 1945, the *News Letter* reported that Roberts, 'whose Home Guard case was given great publicity and called forth an historical comment from the Liverpool Recorder', had returned safely to his home in Antigua.[3]

20

Flying Bombs

Throughout the war there had been fears that the Germans would start using a 'secret weapon' but it wasn't until summer 1944 that it became a reality. The first flying bombs landed on 13 June, seven days after the D-Day invasion of Europe, which had lifted the spirits of the people. The Germans started to send pilotless flying bombs over the English Channel. They were the deadly V-1s, better known as doodlebugs or 'buzz bombs'. The engine had a low, humming sound and, when it cut out, the bomb fell to the ground and caused much death and destruction. They gave very little warning to potential victims. As Juliet Gardiner wrote in *Wartime: Britain 1939–1945*:

> That first weekend of the attack was the worst. Although many bombs crashed on take-off, or failed to make it across the Channel, a steady stream was reaching the capital … The congregation of the Guards Chapel of Wellington Barracks in Birdcage Walk, just around the corner from Buckingham Palace, had just stood to sing … when a V-1 hit the building. In all, fifty-eight civilians and sixty-three service personnel were killed, and nearly seventy people seriously injured.[1]

Between June and September 1944, 9,000 flying bombs killed more than 6,000 people. Those who lived through the period recalled it as more terrifying than the Blitz. In 1944, Pauline Henebery (see Chapter 1) was living with her young daughter Gail in her sister Eunice's flat in Chalk Farm, north London. She described the 'doodlebombs' as:

> ... very alarming. I didn't like them at all, but one just got on with it. I don't remember feeling fear, partly because I was so busy. I was working. We had to cope with the bombing, which was disturbing. I couldn't bear going into the shelters.

Eunice had a Morrison shelter in her house. This was an indoor cage that was designed to protect occupants from masonry and debris if the house was hit by a bomb. Pauline said:

> Eunice insisted on sleeping in this with her daughter and Gail. It was big enough for all of us, but I couldn't stand it. I spent two nights in it, and then I said no, I'd rather have the bombs. So I went back to my own bed and left Gail with Eunice.[2]

Gail, who was 7 years old at the time, didn't share her mother's alarm:

> As doodle-bugs whined overhead, [cousin] Juliet and I slept in a metal bomb shelter which I thought was very cosy and enjoyable. We played with our Christmas presents and told each other stories to take our minds away from the bombs.[3]

Roi Ottley was an African American journalist who, in 1944, was commissioned as a lieutenant in the US Army. He was then sent to Europe to report on the war for several American journals including *Liberty Magazine*, *PM* and the *Pittsburgh Courier*. Ottley became the first African American war correspondent to cover the war for major newspapers. His war diary, published in 2011, revealed a great deal about life in Britain in 1944–45. On 19 July 1944, he wrote:

Last night I spent the most miserable and frightening night of my life. The 'Buzz bombs' were coming over London at the rate of one every ten minutes. The Nazis started sending them over at midnight continuously until about 10 A.M. Next morning I lay in bed unable to sleep all night listening to the crash, crash, crash – wondering! At least three of them hit within two blocks of our flat and shook the house until the building seemed as though it would fall apart. I frankly was never so scared. I thought my time was up. Unless one has experienced these raids, he has no idea how demoralizing they can be.[4]

It was unsettling to hear the approaching, unmistakable drone, then listen for the engine to cut out – which meant that it would immediately drop. Morale hit an all-time low for the first time since 1940. Fulham resident Esther Bruce recalled:

When I heard it I knew I was safe, but when the engine stopped I wondered where it was going to drop. It was really frightening because they killed thousands of people and a lot of them dropped on Fulham. As soon as the engine cut out I'd say: 'Oh, God, it's stopped. Where am I going?' I'd lay down in the kerb or wherever I was and waited for it to explode. I'd just lay down and hope and pray it wasn't going to go off there.[5]

Air-raid wardens recorded that thirteen doodlebugs fell on Fulham between 18 June and 2 August 1944. Leslie Hasker in *Fulham in the Second World War* commented:

The last of the flying-bombs in Fulham, and in fact the last incident in the Borough for the entire war, was at Beaumont Crescent at twenty minutes before midnight on Wednesday

August 2. Seven people were killed and twenty-seven seriously injured. There was considerable damage.[6]

Esther remembered the incident, which she described as 'terrible' because it also demolished some of the houses in Dieppe Street which backed onto Beaumont Crescent:

I remember one terrible incident with a doodlebug that really frightened us. The air-raid sirens warned us that doodlebugs were on their way so off we went to the shelter. We were waiting in the shelter for the all-clear when suddenly there was a terrific explosion and the shelter shook. A doodlebug had fallen on Beaumont Crescent and damaged some of the houses in Dieppe Street. Some people were killed and many were left injured and homeless. Luckily our house was alright, even though it was number thirteen. We called it 'lucky thirteen' after that! At first the air raid warden wouldn't let us go back home because it wasn't safe. They'd hit the gas mains. So, we all had to go to the Lillie Road Rest Centre and stay there until it was safe to return to our homes.[7]

According to the air-raid warden's report of the incident, 200 people were admitted to the Lillie Road Rest Centre. Four houses had been demolished, and many seriously damaged. There had been widespread damage in the area but nearby North End Road was clear.[8]

On 8 September 1944, the arrival of another, deadlier 'secret weapon' instilled more terror. The V-2 rocket, the Germans' second long-range bomb, was massive: 46ft long and 5ft in diameter at the widest part, which carried about a ton of explosives. It moved faster than the speed of sound, so there was no warning for its victims. The noise of the V-2 was ear-splitting. It sounded like a thunderclap followed by a blinding blue flash. Then a roaring sound could be heard for up to 10 miles as the rocket descended.

Thirty-six V-2s landed in September 1944, and 131 in October. They mostly fell on London, but the death toll was less than that caused by the doodlebugs: in total 2,754 people were killed by the V-2s as compared to 6,184 by the V-1s, and 6,523 were injured. There was no defence against them. Juliet Gardiner said:

> Their terror lay in unpredictability, and their dreadful impact. A single V-2 could cause a crater as large as 50 feet wide and 10 feet deep. A row of perhaps thirty terrace houses in the vicinity of the rocket bomb would be virtually razed.[9]

Following his assessment of the doodlebugs, Roi Ottley reported in his diary on 10 October 1944:

> A new terror weapon has been unleashed by the Nazis – V-2, which is a rocket bomb. It seems impossible to stop it. The fact is, no one knows what time of day or night it will hit. For it comes over silently, even stealthily. It is even worse than the buzz bomb because it sneaks into London and no one seems to know where they are being launched from now that the Allies have the whole French coast. It makes a bigger crater than the buzz bombs and a louder noise. Officially the correspondents cannot report its existence. The censors say this ruling is for security reasons – but certainly the Germans know what damage they are doing in London – actually they are raising havoc. Since they have been coming over, there have been no air raid alerts. You can only hope and pray that one doesn't have your name on it.[10]

The Trinidadian folk singer Edric Connor had only recently arrived in Britain, He was lodging with an elderly couple, Mr and Mrs Thomas Bunt, at 39 Capel Gardens in Ilford, Essex. He described them as his 'English parents':

> Every morning I ran two to three miles around Barking Park. Came the morning of 18 December 1944. I put on

my togs. Wearily. Went downstairs. Lazily. Opened the door. Apprehensively. Went to the gate and turned back into the house. Five minutes later the explosion of a rocket occurred somewhere over Upminster. I began to count slowly. One. Two. Three. And the most awful explosion roared on Longbridge Road, at the foot of Capel Gardens. The house swayed. The blast ripped the glass from all the windows. All the pictures left the walls. My bed was in another corner of the room. The rocket dug a thirty-foot crater just at the point where I would have been had I gone for my exercise. Thirteen people were killed in the houses nearby. Five of them could not be identified. I would have disappeared without trace.[11]

On Saturday, 25 November 1944, Dr Harold Moody left his surgery in Queen's Road, Peckham, to attend the aftermath of a V-2 rocket incident in New Cross Road. This was in the very heart of working-class Deptford in south-east London. It wasn't far from where he worked, and Dr Moody was one of the first on the scene where 168 people were killed and more than 120 were seriously injured, mainly mothers and their children who were among the Christmas shopping crowds.

Dr Moody attended as part of a team called in from the surrounding area. They struggled night and day amidst the chaos and carnage to bring comfort to the survivors. It is likely that George A. Roberts, the Trinidad-born fireman based at nearby New Cross Fire Station, would have attended the scene also.

The missile fell at 12.26 p.m. to the rear of Woolworths in New Cross Road. Eyewitnesses later said that the store, which was full of women and children, bulged slightly outwards and then collapsed inwards in a huge cloud of dust and smoke which mushroomed high into the air. Norman Longmate said:

To anyone watching it must have seemed as if Woolworths had been struck by a giant hammer, followed by a volcano-like eruption of rubble and bodies flung skyward, before they sank, slowly it seemed, back to earth, landing with a series of clatters and crashes. Then, as the last of these died away, there seemed to be a moment of silence, before it was broken by the screams and groans of the dying and injured, invisible beneath the tall column of dust that hung over the mound of shattered brick and timber that a minute earlier had been a busy store, and the sobs and cries of frightened children calling for their mothers ... Everyone in New Cross knew what a sudden explosion meant.[12]

Those inside Woolworths did not stand a chance. Next door, the Co-op was also reduced to rubble, killing more people. Passers-by were lifted into the air by the blast and thrown about the area like rag dolls. Parked cars and delivery vans burst into flames. Damaged shops and houses stretched from New Cross Gate station to Deptford Town Hall.

After the explosion, eyewitnesses recalled seeing scores of dazed and blood-covered victims sitting on the pavements or running away hysterically. Some were silent and motionless; others lay dead on the pavements and in the road. The air was filled with grit and dust. There was a huge crater on the site of Woolworths where the V-2 had fallen.

This was the horrific scene that met Dr Moody and the emergency services when they arrived. At night, flood lights were set up to enable the rescuers to continue through the hours of darkness. They toiled hard for two days and nights before their arduous task was done. Despite their efforts, eleven bodies were never found. It was Britain's worst disaster in the entire V-1 and V-2 weapon campaign.[13]

21

Front-Line Films

Cinema played an important role during the Second World War. In addition to films being produced for morale-boosting entertainment, there were films made for propaganda and shown at home and in the colonies. Commercial and propaganda films created an important space for black people.

In the 1930s, the charismatic American expatriate Paul Robeson was the first black actor to attain stardom in British cinema. Though he disowned his first British film, Alexander Korda's *Sanders of the River* (1935), for its imperialism, Robeson found British filmmakers more accommodating than those in America. Top billing in films like *Song of Freedom* (1936), *King Solomon's Mines* (1937) and *Jericho* (1937) helped establish Robeson as a box office attraction in Britain, but he described *The Proud Valley* (1940) as 'the one film I could be proud of having played in'. However, the outbreak of the Second World War ended his British movie career when, along with other American expatriates, he returned home.

The script for *The Proud Valley*, from a treatment by the left-wing Herbert Marshall and his wife, Alfredda Brilliant, enabled Robeson to express his socialist beliefs and portray the struggles of the working-class people of South Wales. For Robeson, making *The Proud Valley* was a rewarding experience, both on and off camera. His biographer, Marie Seton, described how the Welsh people embraced Robeson and took him to their hearts:

> They knew he was a great singer. That meant a lot to them for music was as deep a part of their heritage as it was of his: but it seemed they found something else in him; the decency and simplicity of their own folk.[1]

War broke out in the middle of filming and the production closed down for a couple of days. As an American citizen, Robeson could have packed his bags and departed for America with his family there and then, but he was committed to the film. When filming resumed, he remained in Britain until *The Proud Valley* was finished. In a memoir of his father, *The Undiscovered Paul Robeson*, Paul Robeson Jr recalled how his parents coped:

> Essie [his mother] drove Paul for the thirty-minute trip back and forth to the studio. The exercise became quite a problem when Paul had to work late, since the blackout rules often forced Essie to drive home in almost pitch darkness. Somehow, she always managed.[2]

The Proud Valley was completed on 25 September and three days later Paul and Essie saw a rough cut of the film. The Robeson's were thrilled, and on 30 September they boarded the USS *Washington* at Southampton for the journey home to New York. On 25 February 1940, *The Proud Valley* became the first film to be premiered on radio. That evening, the BBC broadcast a sixty-minute version of the film, reproduced from its soundtrack, on their Home Service.

The closure of film studios, and the dramatic fall in film production during the war years, made it almost impossible for black artistes to work in the medium. Only a select few appeared, and these were mostly singers who were featured in musical sequences, such as Adelaide Hall in Alexander Korda's *The Thief of Bagdad* (1940), the Jamaican baritone Uriel Porter in *He Found a Star* (1941), Elisabeth Welch in *This Was Paris* and *Alibi* (both 1942) and Leslie 'Hutch' Hutchinson in *Happidrome* (1943).

Films with a wartime setting (and there were quite a few), such as Noel Coward's critically acclaimed *In Which We Serve* (1942), failed to acknowledge the existence of black service personnel, but they did inspire some West Indian men to join up, such as the Jamaican Eddie Martin Noble (see Chapter 14). In the melo-drama *2,000 Women* (1944), a small group of black women and children can be glimpsed among the British female inmates of a German internment camp in France.

In December 1942, following discussions between the Colonial Office and the Ministry of Defence, Two Cities Films asked the army to release the renowned director Thorold Dickinson from making military training films. They wanted him to direct a film they considered to be of 'national importance'. Dickinson was asked to make a film about East Africa. He said, 'It was not to be a spectacle of conquest or a documentary, but an intimate dramatic study of the two races working side by side.'[3]

Pre-production on *Men of Two Worlds* was long and compli-cated. The central character, Kisenga, an East African composer and pianist played by Robert Adams, was introduced at the beginning of the story taking part in a lunchtime concert at the National Gallery in London's Trafalgar Square. However, Dame Myra Hess, who organised almost 2,000 lunchtime concerts at the gallery throughout the war, insisted that it was inconceivable that a black man would be capable of composing music of a qual-ity good enough to be played there and refused to allow filming on location. So, Dickinson recreated the interior and exterior of the gallery in a film studio and the scene was filmed.

Problems also arose with the West African Students' Union (WASU), an influential political organisation based in London. They were happy to consult on the script, until they were sent a copy. Their response was highly critical. While they recognised the film could be used as helpful propaganda, they objected to the depiction of a villainous witch doctor. In July 1943, WASU's executive committee passed a resolution, which it enclosed with a letter of protest to the Colonial Office, stating that the script 'casts a slur on the prestige of African peoples as a whole' and 'prejudices future relations between the African peoples and the British Empire'. They stated that there was no such thing as a witch doctor in African law and custom, 'It is entirely a European invention.'[4] In spite of script revisions, when *Men of Two Worlds* was released after the war, in 1946, it was a critical and box office failure.

The large numbers of African American GIs in wartime Britain drew attention to the escalating problem of racist attacks up and down the country from white American GIs. Consequently, a documentary film called *Welcome to Britain* was commissioned by the War Office from the Ministry of Information (MOI) to address this problem. It was then handed over to the American Office of War Information for distribution among American troops.

Released in December 1943, *Welcome to Britain*, devised and directed by one of Britain's most respected filmmakers, Anthony Asquith, was intended as a 'guide' to British behaviour for newly arrived American troops stationed in the UK. The American actor Burgess Meredith, then a captain in the American army, acted as the film's on-screen guide and narrator. The purpose of the film was to show American GIs how to get along with the British people. In one sequence, the comedian Bob Hope 'explained' the British currency system. Graham Smith commented in *When Jim Crow Met John Bull* (1987):

> It included a quite remarkable sequence on race, asking the American soldiers to respect the different attitudes they would find in Britain. In effect the film granted the request that [John L.] Keith of the Colonial Office, amongst others, had wanted

all along – the right to inform the Americans of the British view on this matter.[5]

In *Welcome to Britain*, Burgess Meredith spoke directly to the camera and informed white GIs:

> There are less social restrictions in this country … You heard an Englishwoman asking a coloured boy to tea. She was polite about it and he was polite about it. Now … look; that might not happen at home but the point is, we're not at home.

West Indies Calling (1943) was a short documentary film made by the independent producer Paul Rotha for the MOI. During the Second World War, the Films Division of the MOI was responsible for film propaganda in Britain. They assumed control of the GPO (General Post Office) Film Unit (renamed the Crown Film Unit) for the production of official documentaries.

Rotha's film showed how West Indians in Britain were involved in the war effort. It featured the Jamaican broadcaster Una Marson at the BBC's Broadcasting House studio in London, hosting a broadcast to the Caribbean with two Trinidadians, Learie Constantine and Flying Officer Ulric Cross. They described to listeners of *Calling the West Indies*, the popular BBC Radio series, how people from the Caribbean were supporting the war effort.

Constantine spoke about factory workers, and introduced some war workers, including Cross, a bomber navigator. Cross told of his work in the RAF and spoke about some of the 10,000 volunteers for the armed services from the Caribbean. Representing 900 lumberjacks, Carlton Fairweather talked about forestry work by lumbermen from British Honduras.

Although the introductions and commentaries sound stilted at times, the film footage that accompanied it provided some rare screen images of black participation in the Second World War. These included service personnel such as fighter pilots, engineers, factory workers, lumberjacks and nurses. The film ended with a dance in a BBC studio and much emphasis was given to co-operation between peoples of different national and racial backgrounds.

The Colonial Film Unit (CFU) was a documentary production company founded in 1939 as part of the MOI to make films of special interest to audiences in what was then the British Empire. Its films were distributed by the Colonial Office of Information. Film was to be in the 'front line' of war propaganda. In 1957, the director George Pearson commented that the establishment of the CFU 'was tangible recognition of the potential power of the screen … The films were shown to native audiences by travelling cinema vans that penetrated deep into the African interior, far from the populated coast towns.'[6]

The function of the CFU's films was essentially that of education and propaganda. Between its birth in 1939 and closure in 1955, the CFU produced a total of 280 short films, and eighty-five of these were war related. The original purpose of the CFU was to explain the war to audiences in the colonies, to tell them why Britain was fighting and invite their support.

The CFU produced and distributed a number of goodwill films in which they tried to persuade colonial African audiences that they were involved in the war. The CFU requested the production of films that showed how Africans were integrating into the British way of life. For example, in 1941 George Pearson directed *An African in London*, which showed a West African, portrayed by Robert Adams, being given a short tour of London landmarks. The purpose of the film was to show African audiences that everyone was a member of the British Empire and 'that all may look to the imperial centre, that all are welcome there, and that there is opportunity for all irrespective of race or creed'.[7]

West African Editors (1944) showed a group of West African journalists, including Nnamdi Azikiwe, editor of the journal *West African Pilot*, on a visit to Britain. Another theme from the CFU was gratitude for the support the colonies in West Africa were giving to the war effort. *Katsina Tank* (1943), featuring the London-based Nigerian air-raid warden E.I. Ekpenyon, showed how gifts from the colonies were being used in Britain.

From 1943 to 1945, a monthly 16mm silent newsreel called *The British Empire at War*, designed for showing in mobile cinema vans, was added to the CFU's repertoire. It ran to twenty-five editions and included two directed by George Pearson in 1943: *Nurse Ademola* and *Pilot Officer Peter Thomas*, who, in 1941, was the first commissioned Nigerian in the RAF.

The Caribbean was not overlooked. Learie Constantine was the subject of the CFU's *Learie Constantine* (1944), also directed by George Pearson, for distribution in the British West Indies. *Learie Constantine* showed the day-to-day work of Constantine, meeting factory workers, listening to their problems and taking part in a charity cricket match. The film was silent, and it would have been shown to audiences in venues without sound equipment. The MOI was quick to realise that there was great propaganda value in the fact that Constantine, known as a famous cricketer, was deeply involved in a vital wartime task, helping to integrate West Indians into British society and the workforce.

Regrettably, most of the CFU's wartime output has been lost, including *An African in London*, *Katsina Tank* and *Nurse Ademola*, but prints of *Pilot Officer Peter Thomas* (in a compilation entitled *Africa's Fighting Men*, 1943) and *Learie Constantine* have survived.

22

Mother Country

In 1939, many people in power in Britain viewed the West African, Guyanese and Caribbean colonies as backwaters of the British Empire, but when war was declared on Germany, the people of the empire immediately rallied behind the 'mother country'. In spite of the poverty and exploitation they experienced, many people growing up in the empire were, said Guyana's Randolph Beresford, 'more British than the British. As a boy, we celebrated Queen Victoria's birthday. We were told we were a part of Britain, we were British.'[1]

Many black people from the across the empire supported the British war effort because they saw the possibility of post-war reform and independence for their homelands. Others were motivated by a sense of duty to overcome the struggle between the so-called 'free world' and fascism. The people of the empire strongly identified with the mother country and wanted to protect their homelands from Nazi occupation.

In Jamaica, Sam King was keen to support the British, 'I don't think the British Empire was perfect, but it was better than Nazi Germany. So I wanted to join the armed service.' In 1944 Sam joined the RAF.[2]

However, Austin Clarke has given a more cynical account of how some West Indian islanders felt. Describing the sudden changes in life on the island of Barbados, which was also known as 'Little England', he said:

All of a sudden we had an army. The police were put on alert. Sea scouts became self-important, as they were taken deeper out into the harbour and told a few things about spotting enemy ships by the harbour police. And we heard that our leader, Grantley Adams, sent a cable up to the King, and told the King, 'Go on, England, Little England is behind you.' We were English. The allegiance and the patriotism that our leader, Mr Grantley Adams, had imprisoned us with had been cabled to the Colonial Office in London. We were the English of Little England. Little black Englishmen.[3]

Wartime restrictions and German U-boats patrolling the Atlantic and Caribbean islands brought the war to the remotest parts of the British Empire. Trinidad was considered one of the most vulnerable islands in the West Indies because it was a major source of oil and was a supply base for the British. It was in Trinidad that Calypsonians mocked Hitler and Nazi Germany with their songs including Lord Beginner's 'Run Your Run Hitler'.

People living in Caribbean islands such as Barbados, Jamaica, Montserrat, Grenada and Trinidad experienced a war not dissimilar to that of the mother country. They shared some of the conditions of life on the home front in Britain. Home Guards units were organised, and air-raid drills and blackout routines were carried out.

There were fears that the Germans might attack, so they had air-raid sirens to warn people of possible attacks and introduced blackout regulations, air-raid precautions and employed air-raid wardens to enforce the rules. The wardens often visited towns and villages on the islands to see if anyone was breaking the rules by showing any light that might attract possible bombers.

However, when the Guyanese actor Norman Beaton recalled the war in his autobiography, he described his father's role as an air-raid warden as:

> ... a totally useless exercise. Not one single plane ever came near Georgetown, and when it was rumoured that a torpedo had been discovered on the beach, the whole of Georgetown rushed down to the sea wall to have a look at the devilish engine.[4]

Food and water rationing was also introduced. In addition to newspapers providing readers in the colonies with information, local government information departments also published and distributed news sheets, and these were especially important in the smaller islands of the Caribbean, which lacked a newspaper of their own. Propaganda in the form of poster campaigns and films produced by the CFU played an important role in gaining support and recruiting civilians across the empire for the war effort.

In Jamaica there was an internment camp for German and Italian prisoners of war. German U-boats patrolling the Caribbean islands attacked passenger ships and destroyed shipping. Vital freight was destroyed, contributing to the shortages of basic commodities. An increase in the production of oil and bauxite in the West Indies drew German U-boats into American shipping lanes.

In 1942, a Canadian ship called the *Cornwallis* was docked in Barbados Harbour when a German U-boat hit it and sank it with torpedoes. The explosion could be heard right across Barbados and the islanders prepared for a German invasion. Austin Clarke has described the panic that followed:

> All of a sudden people were running for their lives. They were in cars, on bicycles, and some were in donkey carts. The Germans had invaded Barbados ... We had been content to read about the war in the *Advocate*, in the photographs in the

few copies of *Life* magazine that trickled into the island, in *Movietone* newsreels at the Empire Theatre, and every night on the BBC. This afternoon the people were running for the hills ... The Germans were coming, the men said ... and the island would be put in a concentration camp. We had heard about concentration camps on the BBC. And as in all other ways of life in the island, who got to the hills first were the rich people. During the war, the rich people were the white people. After the war the black people laughed at the white people for getting to the hills first. They were 'blasted cowards,' the black people said. 'More blasted cowards than we poor people!'[5]

Just a few hours later, it became apparent that the Germans were not going to land in Barbados after all. 'They had just stopped by to torpedo a ship,' said Austin Clarke.[6]

In spite of being a small and impoverished part of the British Empire, the people and governments of the Caribbean offered substantial assistance to the British war effort. Some of this was reported in the wartime newsletters of the LCP. As early as September 1940, Dr Harold Moody reported that in the British Colonial Empire of '60,000,000 souls', 44 million were to be found in Africa and the West Indies:

[They] have subscribed over nine million pounds sterling, besides much goods, to Britain's war effort. Of this vast amount nearly one million pounds sterling, in addition to valuable produce and hospital supplies, have come from the impoverished people of the West Indies. It must be recognised that our people have made these incredible sacrifices, not only because of their love for Britain, but even more because they know something of what slavery means, and as human beings they are lovers of liberty.[7]

23

VE Day

Tuesday, 8 May 1945 was VE – Victory in Europe – Day. Germany had surrendered. It was the end of the war in Europe. It was a time for celebration, but it was also a time for reflection. On VE Day, a jubilant crowd of thousands made their way to Buckingham Palace in London. They clamoured for the royal family. King George VI and Queen Elizabeth, with the two princesses, Elizabeth and Margaret, went out on the palace balcony eight times. Prime Minister Winston Churchill joined the royal family on the balcony. That day he told the nation, 'My dear friends, this is your hour. This is not victory of a party or of any class. It's a victory of the great British nation as a whole.'

Far away in Germany, Adelaide Hall was in the middle of her ENSA tour. She was in Hamburg when she was notified that the war had ended. Adelaide then became one of the first entertainers to arrive in Berlin to congratulate the troops after the city had been liberated. She said:

There was not a street in sight – nothing. They had all been razed to the ground, and people were putting up little boards, made from bits of wood, to identify the names of the streets that used to be there.[1]

After the war, her husband Bert couldn't get her out of the uniform specially made for her by Madame Adele of Grosvenor Street. He told his wife, 'The war is over now, honey, you can let that uniform go!'

Norma Best, from British Honduras, had joined the ATS in 1944. She was in London for VE Day and took part in the end-of-war celebrations on the Embankment. She later reflected:

> I think the spirit of the war was that we were all fighting to win. All we could think about is to get in there, do a good job, let's get it over and done with. Colour didn't come into it.[2]

In January 1945, the newsletter of the LCP noted that Ulric Cross had been appointed the first liaison officer for West Indians in the RAF. They added that the recent award of the Distinguished Service Order (DSO) to Ulric was 'a joy to every West Indian heart'. Ulric heard on the radio that the war was over, and he went to Piccadilly Circus in London to join the celebrations:

> Everybody was overjoyed and I just didn't feel like taking any part in it. So I went back home. I just felt that a lot of people had been killed. This was not a cause for celebration. The war did not stop people from being killed and a lot of my friends were killed, at least four or five from Trinidad. I was extremely glad the war was over.[3]

In Jamaica, Connie Mark, who was serving with the ATS, remembered VE Day as a marvellous time:

> Everybody was happy 'cause as far as we were concerned, the war was finished. Everybody was happy. Everybody just

jumped up and down; the war was over, and it meant that no more of our people would be killed. We had parties, and everybody took it as an excuse to have a party, a drink up, and get stone-blind drunk. I didn't used to drink in those days; I just went to all the parties that there were. Yeah, you were glad that the war was over, and people weren't going to die. You didn't have troop ships coming in with people sick, or blinded, or with missing limbs.[4]

Cerene Palmer said that everybody in Jamaica wanted to know that Hitler was really dead. 'They wanted to make sure it was him. They hung Mussolini so everybody could see him. You knew he was dead.'[5]

In England, another Jamaican, Sam King, was at his RAF hangar, repairing an aircraft, when victory was announced on the tannoy. Everyone was given the remainder of the day off, but they were told they would have to be back on duty the next day. Sam put on his RAF uniform and caught the bus into Weston-super-Mare:

It was different. The birds were singing. I got off the bus and I was on the right-hand side of the road, passing the George and Dragon. A lady rushed out: 'Come along! You must have a drink.' She pulled me in the pub and said, 'Bring rum for this airman, he's from Jamaica.' I said, 'I'm very sorry. I do not drink rum.' She said, 'How can you not drink rum? You've got Jamaica on your shoulder!' She brought the rum and I had to drink the rum. Everybody was happy. It was VE Day. There'll be no more bombing. No more killing. And especially for the women whose loved ones were coming home. It was good to be alive and I was alive.[6]

Harold Sinson, from British Guiana, served in the RAF in Pembroke Dock in Wales. When asked about his memories of VE Day, he spoke of how everyone just downed tools:

Everything was free – there were drinks all over the place, there was dancing in the street. It was really exciting. It lasted all that day and all night – nobody knew what was happening, you just danced away until you had enough and you went back to camp and to bed. We got off the next day – it was wonderful. We spent time with our friends, and felt very humble for the things people did for us and the people who had died.[7]

Eddie Martin Noble was a Jamaican who was also in the RAF and serving in England. He said he was in Cambridge on VE Day when 'the very the end of the war in Europe was announced'. In his autobiography, published in 1984, he reflected:

It is almost impossible for me to adequately describe here, after all these years, the incredible scenes of joy and sheer abandonment which took place in Cambridge that day and night. Complete strangers would hug and kiss you in the streets, shops and parks. There was dancing in the streets, and bonfires everywhere. In a park near the university I saw servicemen and officers take off their tunics and throw them on a massive bonfire.[8]

Eddie acknowledged that Winston Churchill was 'a great war leader'. He believed that, without his leadership, the British people would have lost the war, 'But, to put it bluntly, he was a bastard. As soon as the war ended they threw him out, and let a Labour government in, so that should tell you something.'[9]

On VE Day, the Trinidadian singer Edric Connor was ready to broadcast the first instalment of a new BBC series of programmes called *Serenade in Sepia*. However, the live broadcast was postponed so that the BBC could do justice to the celebrations of the end of the war. It was decided that Edric and his co-star, Evelyn Dove, would record the programme on VE Day instead and it would be broadcast at a later date. However, getting to Broadcasting House on VE Day proved an almost impossible task for Edric:

Most public transport stopped running. Housewives left kitchens. Shops and schools were closed. All commercial and industrial activities ceased. The only way I could get to London that day was in a hearse. As I sat near the coffin I contemplated the dead body it contained. What a day to go to the BBC! Then I thought of the millions of people killed in the war and wept quietly. Somebody has to cry for the steel that is bent and the body broken against its will. Somebody has to cry for the children unborn and those born but hungry. Somebody had to cry for humanity. The hearse put me down at Oxford Circus.[10]

Ambrose Campbell, the Nigerian musician and bandleader, was also drawn into the VE Day celebrations. On that memorable day he launched his new band, the West African Rhythm Brothers, in Trafalgar Square and Piccadilly Circus. Sixty years later, Campbell reflected:

Everybody had been waiting for that day so everybody was happy and jumping around and dancing and kissing each other, so we thought we'd join the celebration. Four or five drummers and two or three guitars and these voices singing. We had a huge crowd following us around Piccadilly Circus. You could hardly move.[11]

In *Black London*, Marc Matera described Campbell's participation in VE Day as a 'spontaneous expression of hope for a transformed post-war social order'.[12]

As the war drew to a close, Dr Harold Moody made a broadcast to the people of the Caribbean for the BBC's Empire Service in their series, *Calling the West Indies*. Extracts were then published in the *News Letter* of the LCP. 'VE Day has come and gone,' he said:

The years of blood and toil and sweat have come to an end in Europe. The tension of war for millions is over. We are free again in the continent of Europe. I have been in the midst of a peoples whose homes have been shattered, whose families have been battered, who themselves have been maimed. I have seen these people bear all these shocks bravely and with stoic resistance. I now see these same people breathing the air of relief, and, in their rejoicing, lighting those fires the sight of which, a while ago, would have struck them with terror ... I have rejoiced in meeting from time to time the fine group of men and women you have sent over from the West Indies, British Guiana and British Honduras. Their doings and achievements have thrilled me beyond telling. They will be coming back to you, we hope, before very long now, just as I hope my five boys and girls in the services will be back again soon. They have all done magnificently as they battled against evil things. Now they and you will have to continue the war against those evil things which are hindering the progress and development of our beloved lands in the West Indies.[13]

On 24 April 1947, at the age of 64, Dr Moody died of acute influenza at his home in Peckham. Thousands of people from all walks of life, including many of his patients, paid their respects at his funeral service which was held at the Camberwell Green Congregational Church.

In his biography of Dr Moody, David A. Vaughan described him as the leader of his people in the mother country and revealed that, during the war, he never neglected the easily forgotten small communities of black people living in seaport towns. For example, a group of 200 Africans had been stranded in Newcastle at the start of the war, and they were often lonely and unhappy because of their feeling of isolation from the social life of the local community. Following an appeal from them, in 1941 Dr Moody travelled to Newcastle and met with a group of eleven representatives including the Nigerian community leader Charles Minto. The group derived much benefit and encouragement from Moody's visit.

Vaughan added that Moody gave to the LCP 'devotion, sacrifice, passion and zeal for the rest of his life and he held the office of President continuously until his death in 1947'. Sam Morris commented, 'In his passing, the black people then resident in Britain lost a sound, sincere, dedicated but completely unpretentious champion.'[14]

***

Pauline Henebery remembered the feeling of relief when the war in Europe was over, but it was short-lived for her because of the shock of what happened to Hiroshima, a city in Japan that was largely destroyed by an atomic bomb on 6 August 1945. Between 70,000 and 126,000 civilians were killed. She said:

> I remember the news of that, and was just shattered by the horror, and what it was going to mean. It was just so, so awful. I had the most terrible feeling of guilt that this nation which I'd adopted had done this … well, it was the Americans, really, but still.[15]

Baron Baker, a Jamaican who had joined the RAF in 1944, felt passionately about the role West Indian servicemen had played in the conflict, as well as the sacrifices some of them had made for the mother country:

> Many of our blue blood blacks died for the establishment. I know it because I buried several … so many of our young Jamaicans, and West Indians, contributed immensely to Britain's war effort. It should be remembered at all times. It should never be forgotten.[16]

At the end of the war, Esther Bruce took Stephen Bourne's mother Kathy, aged 14, to see St Paul's Cathedral. Like so many others, Esther found it hard to believe that St Paul's had survived the German bombardment of London (the Blitz, doodlebugs and V-2 rockets). For many, including Esther, the beautiful and majestic cathedral symbolised the hope and strength of the British people. 'Look at St. Paul's Cathedral,' Esther said to Kathy. 'There's not a mark on it. We're lucky. We've still got half a street, but some poor souls have ended up with nothing.'

★★★

Meanwhile, in 1944, the liberation of Paris was a military battle that took place from 19 August until the Germans surrendered the French capital on 25 August. Soon afterwards, the Guyanese conductor Rudolph Dunbar presented a Festival of American Music in the Théâtre des Champs-Elysées in Paris with the Conservatoire Orchestra. The programme included the premiere of *In Memoriam: The Colored Soldiers Who Died for Democracy* by the African American composer, William Grant Still.

In 1942 Dunbar had made his London conducting debut with the London Philharmonic at the Royal Albert Hall to an audience of 7,000 people. In addition to his concert career, Dunbar was a journalist who, during the war, had worked as the London correspondent for the Associated Negro Press news agency in the USA. As a war correspondent, he served with the American Eighth Army, and crossed the English Channel on D-Day, 6 June 1944, with a black regiment. He distinguished himself by warning the US 969th Battalion of an ambush during the Battle of the Bulge.

In September 1945, Dunbar conducted the Berlin Philharmonic. In America, the popular magazine *Time* reported on this historic occasion:

At a concert this week ... Berlin's famed 65-year-old Philharmonic Orchestra was led by a war correspondent in battledress. The guest conductor was a Negro, born in British Guiana. The 2,000 Berliners and the 500 Allied soldiers in the audience found it quite an experience. They applauded warmly when the conductor led the orchestra through Weber's familiar *Oberon* and Tchaikovsky's *Pathétique*. They broke into cheers, and called him back five times, when he gave them Berlin's first hearing of fellow-Negro William Grant Still's boisterous, bluesy *Afro-American Symphony*.[17]

Time added that the presence of Rudolph Dunbar and his outstanding musicianship had taught the German people a lesson in racial tolerance.

If Hitler Had Invaded

Holocaust Memorial Day, held every February, was mainly set up to remember the 6 million Jewish men, women and children murdered by Hitler's Nazi regime and, while a great deal of information has been documented about Jewish victims, the Nazis' persecution and murder of other groups is still to be fully researched and acknowledged. It has been estimated that at least another 5 million 'others' could have perished in Nazi concentration camps and these would have included communists, lesbians, gays, Jehovah's Witnesses, gypsies, and people with physical or mental disabilities.

According to the United States Holocaust Memorial Museum in Washington DC:

> The fate of black people from 1933 to 1945 in Nazi Germany and in German-occupied territories ranged from isolation to persecution, sterilization, medical experimentation, incarceration, brutality and murder. However, there was no systematic program for their elimination as there was for Jews and other groups.[1]

When Hitler was the ruler of Germany (1933–45), many black and mixed-race Germans were rounded up by the Gestapo (the German secret police) and forcibly sterilised. In 1937 local authorities in Germany were asked to submit lists of all children of African descent. These children were taken from their homes or schools without the consent of their parents and, if the child was identified as of African descent, they were taken to a hospital and sterilised. At least 400 mixed-race children were forcibly sterilised in the Rhineland area alone by the end of 1937, while 400 others 'disappeared', probably into Hitler's concentration camps.

It is not known how many people of African descent in Germany and occupied Europe died at the hands of the Nazis during the Holocaust. No records exist. It has been estimated, however, that there were between 20,000 to 25,000 black people living in Germany when Hitler came to power: some were Africans who had travelled from the German colonies; others were French African troops who had settled in Germany after the First World War; some came from other parts of the world and were working or studying in Germany, often as entertainers and musicians. Many of them would have been persecuted, imprisoned, sterilised, brutalised and murdered during the Nazi regime. However, historians of the Second World War have yet to investigate and explore what might have been the fate of Britain's black population if Hitler had invaded.

A German invasion of Britain came very close. After Germany had invaded and occupied France, it was only a matter of time before they crossed the English Channel. Hitler was confident that his plan to invade Britain in September 1940 would be successful and, chillingly, had made arrangements to uproot Nelson's column from Trafalgar Square and erect it in Berlin. In 1972, the historian Norman Longmate gave an absorbing and astonishing account of the effects of a German invasion on Britain in *If Britain Had Fallen*. However, it did not acknowledge the fate of Britain's black population. In a letter to the author in 2006, he explained:

Yours is the first [letter] to ask what would have happened to black UK residents in the event of a successful German invasion. The answer is, I'm afraid, that I cannot be much help. In all the documents on German plans, which cover such matters as the Welsh language, I have not come across any which refer to the presence of people of different colour. I can find no reference to what was then called the colour problem in Martin Kitchen's *Nazi Germany at War* (1995), but I think there is no doubt the Nazi 'master race' philosophy would have dismissed the black races as inferior, indeed they were visibly 'non-Aryan' and the one reference I have found brackets the negroes with the Jews. The Nazis complained about jazz as 'Negroid-Jewish jazz music' as corrupting (Kitchen p.179). Hitler is known to have registered disgust when a black athlete [Jesse Owens] was successful in the 1936 Olympics. To sum up, I think the Nazis gave no particular attention to the black races simply because, unlike the Slavs or the Jews, they were barely visible in Europe. They would, in the event of occupying Britain, have, I think been rounded up but as an afterthought after the Jews, with whom the Nazis were insanely obsessed, had been dealt with.[2]

Some documentation exists about what happened to black Germans under Nazi rule and books written on the subject includes Clarence Lusane's *Hitler's Black Victims* (2002). There is also the inclusion of the African American singer and activist Paul Robeson in Hitler's infamous *Black Book*. Robeson was living in London when the war broke out and the Gestapo had his name in their list of 2,820 British subjects and European and American expatriates living in Britain who were to be automatically arrested following the German invasion of Britain.

Historians of the Second World War have consistently overlooked or avoided the fate of British black people if there had been a German occupation. However, black British citizens, including those in the colonies, were fully aware of what their fate would be if Hitler had invaded. It is because so little attention has been given to this subject their fears have never been reported in the history books or in the media, except on one revealing occasion.

In the television discussion programme *Hear-Say*, shown on BBC 2 in 1990, ex-servicemen and women from the former African and Caribbean colonies debated the pros and cons of supporting the British war effort with members of a younger, more critical generation. Some younger members of the studio audience couldn't understand why black people supported the British when they were forced to live under colonial rule. During the programme the British-born Lilian Bader (see Chapter 16), frustrated with the lack of understanding from some of the younger members of the audience, expressed in no uncertain terms why she had joined the WAAF in 1941, 'We [black people] would have ended up in the ovens.'[3]

If Hitler had invaded England, black British citizens would have been vulnerable. Paul Robeson's inclusion in Hitler's *Black Book* suggests that other prominent black people in Britain, like Dr Harold Moody and Learie Constantine, would also have been arrested and ended up in the hands of the Gestapo. The rest, including my adopted Aunt Esther, would have been rounded up and interned in concentration camps or worse.

Appendix 1: Members of the RAF in Memoriam

The following list includes some of the many RAF personnel who made the ultimate sacrifice.

1942: Pilot Officer Victor Tucker

Pilot Officer (formerly Flight Sergeant) Victor Tucker was a Jamaican of 129 Squadron, RAF Reserve. Before the war he had studied law in England. On 4 May 1942, his Spitfire was shot down in the Channel. The Spitfires were escorting Bostons to Le Havre and aborted the escort shortly before the bombing run. By order they flew a left turn, to which the pilots had protested, as this enabled the Germans to attack from the sun. Victor was just 25 when he made the ultimate sacrifice. He is commemorated on Panel 72 at the Runnymede Memorial in Surrey.

1942: Richard Barr

Richard Eugene Barr was born in Cornwall. His father, Dickie Barr, who was of African descent, was also British-born and served in the First World War. During the Second World War, Richard joined the RAF and served as a sergeant with 149 Squadron. He was killed in action at the age of 29 on 30 June 1942, when his aircraft was shot down and cashed in the Netherlands. He is remembered with honour on the RAF Memorial on Victoria Embankment in London.

1943: Pilot Officer George Nunez

Pilot Officer George Nunez was a Trinidadian of 9 Squadron. His sister, Pearl, came to Britain after the war and married the Trinidadian folk singer, Edric Connor (see Chapters 12, 21 and 24). He was killed in action on 1 May 1943 at the age of 32. He is commemorated on Panel 132 at the Runnymede Memorial in Surrey.

1943: Sergeant Arthur Walrond

Sergeant Arthur Walrond from Barbados served as a wireless operator/air gunner in the RAF Volunteer Reserve. In June 1943, he was based at RAF Mildenhall in Suffolk. At a dance in Bury St Edmunds, Arthur asked a white woman if she would like to dance with him and an American soldier intervened and ordered her not to accept the invitation. In a letter to the Colonial Office dated 29 June 1943, Arthur explained what happened next:

> Despite this, obviously intending to ignore the instruction, she moved towards the dance floor when the same Sergeant attacked me with both fists followed by further assaults from his friend. I had said nothing to him and the attack was made quite suddenly and without provocation. The two soldiers concerned were perfectly sober and there can be no excuse for such an unprovoked assault.

Arthur requested that 'the incident referred to be thoroughly investigated and taken up by the Colonial Office and the people concerned punished'. He concluded, 'I came to this country as a volunteer for air crew duties under the protection of the British government, and I demand as far as is humanly possible that I get that protection.' On the same night he wrote the letter, Arthur, age 29, was killed in action on a bombing raid when his plane was shot down over Belgium by a German night-fighter. He is buried in Heverlee War Cemetery in Belgium.

1943: Sergeant Leslie Gilkes

Sergeant Leslie Gilkes of Trinidad served with 9 Squadron, RAF Volunteer Reserve. He was killed on 3 August 1943. Leslie and his crew were on their ninth mission and were returning home when they were shot down off the coast of Texel, Holland. Leslie, his fellow gunner 'Willie' Welsh and the crew's engineer were never found. He is remembered with honour on Panel 150 at the Runnymede Memorial in Surrey.

1943: Aircraftman 2nd Class Percy Gale

Percy Gale, Aircraftman 2nd Class, RAF Volunteer Reserve, was born in Cardiff, South Wales, and died on 12 August 1943 at the age of 38. He is remembered with honour at the Bone War Cemetery in Annaba in Algeria.

1943: Flying Officer Kenrick Rawlins

Flying Officer Kenrick Rawlins of Trinidad served with 139 Squadron RAF Volunteer Reserve. He was killed in action on 13 August 1943, aged 27. He is remembered with honour on Panel 129 at the Runnymede Memorial in Surrey.

1943: Stafford (Buzz) Barton

Stafford Barton of Jamaica was the son of the news editor of the *Daily Gleaner*. He had been a boxing champion before the war and volunteered for ARP duties in 1939. He served in the RAF Volunteer Reserve with 142 Squadron and was killed in action on 24 November 1943, aged 28, when his plane was shot down over the Mediterranean. He is buried in Staglieno Cemetery, Genoa, Italy.

1944: Pilot Officer Cassian Waight

In 1941 Cassian Waight, a civil servant from Belize City, British Honduras, volunteered for the RAF. In 1944 'Cass' had become a wireless operator/air gunner on a Lancaster with 101 Squadron. He was a member of a crew known as the K for King's 'League of Nations' because, in addition to Cass, they had members from various parts of the British Empire, including South Africa and Canada.

On 6 February 1944, Cass was promoted from sergeant to pilot officer (on probation). In the early hours of 20 February 1944, on a difficult raid on Leipzig in Germany, their Lancaster DV 267 crashed near Tolbert in the northern part of the Netherlands. John 'Jack' Laurens stayed at the controls while it was in its death plunge to give his crew time to get out. Five succeeded, but three were too late, and died. Cass was among them because they had insufficient time to leave the burning Lancaster with their parachutes. 32-year-old Cassian Waight is buried in the Marum (Noordwijk) Protestant churchyard, which is about 12km west of Tolbert in the Netherlands.

1944: Sergeant Bankole Vivour

Sergeant (Air Bomber) Bankole Vivour was described by Roger Lambo in *Africans in Britain* (1994) as a Nigerian bomber who:

> … joined 156 (Pathfinder) Squadron at the height of the winter offensive of 1943–44. On the night of 24–25 March along with 148 other men in the Squadron, he took part in Bomber Command's last determined effort to destroy Berlin. The raid was not a success and the attacking force suffered the loss of 72 bombers. Bankole Vivour survived, to take part in an attack on Essen two nights later. On 30 March 1944, 156 Squadron's Lancasters took off again from their Cambridgeshire base of Upwood. This time the target was Nuremberg deep in the south of Germany. Nuremberg was Bomber Command's most disastrous raid of the entire war. German night-fighters

decimated the attacking force and one of the 545 men who died that night was Sergeant Bankole Vivour. Of his crew of seven men only the pilot survived. Nuremberg effectively marked the end of Air Chief Marshal Arthur Harris's 'Main Offensive' against Germany.

Bankole Vivour was just 24 when he was killed in action on 31 March 1944. He is remembered with honour at the Reichswald Forest War Cemetery in Germany.

1944: Sergeant Vivian Florent

Sergeant Vivian Florent was born in London. He was the son of the St Lucian actor, Napoleon Florent. In 1941 Vivian joined the RAF and two years later he was promoted to sergeant air gunner. He was listed as a flight engineer on a Halifax which took off from RAF Pocklington on 8–9 June 1944, detailed to carry out a gardening mine-laying mission. The aircraft crashed after flying into trees at Home Farm, Seaton Ross, east of the village of Sigglesthorne in Yorkshire. It is possible that the pilot may have lost control when trying to avoid a collision with another aircraft. All the crew were killed and Vivian, aged just 23, was buried in the Pocklington burial ground in Yorkshire.

1944: Flying Officer (Navigator) Gilbert Fairweather

Flying Officer (Navigator) Gilbert Walter Fairweather of 83 Squadron originated from British Honduras and joined the RAF in 1941. He was killed in action on 22 June 1944, at the age of 22. His Lancaster was picked up by a German night-fighter over their target area in Holland and shot down. He is buried with his fellow crew members in the Rheinberg War Cemetery in Germany. Gilbert was awarded the DFC.

1944: Sergeant Arthur Young

Sergeant Arthur Young of 106 Squadron was born in Cardiff and joined the RAF in 1941. On 30 July 1944, he was on a raid over

Normandy but the mission was aborted due to bad visibility. His Lancaster PB 304 returned home with bombs and fuel but it did not reach its base. Somewhere over Manchester, it developed engine trouble and then crashed into the River Irwell in Salford. The full bomb load exploded, and Arthur was killed along with the rest of his seven-man crew. He was just 19. He is remembered with honour on Panel 241 at the Runnymede Memorial in Surrey. In 2019, a memorial was unveiled at the Welsh National War Memorial in Cardiff to remember Sergeant Young and other members of diverse ethnic communities and Commonwealth men and women who served in the two world wars. Arthur's sister, Patti Flynn attended the ceremony.

1944: Warrant Officer James Hyde

Warrant Officer (Pilot) James Hyde, a fighter pilot serving with 132 Squadron, originated from Santa Cruz, San Juan, Trinidad. He was killed in action on 25 September 1944 at the age of 27. He was killed instantly when his aircraft crashed at Elst, near Arnhem, Holland. He is buried in Jonkerbos War Cemetery in the Netherlands.

Appendix 2: Interviews

The following interviews with Loleta Jemmott (Barbados), Olu Richards (Freetown, Sierra Leone), Randol DaCosta (Barbados) and Cerene Palmer (Jamaica) were conducted in the London Borough of Southwark in 2008. The main purpose of the interviews was to explore some of the ways in which the Second World War impacted on the people of the colonies in the Caribbean and West Africa. The similarities with people in the British Isles are the most striking features of the interviews: the threat of a German invasion, children being evacuated, food rationing, blackouts, air-raid warnings and the hatred of Adolf Hitler.

Loleta Jemmott (Barbados)

Loleta Jemmott was born in the parish of St Michael, 1 mile from Bridgetown, the capital of Barbados. She was 6 years old when the war started. 'I can remember the church bells ringing out and people crying out and that was the announcement that the war had started.' Loleta said that during the war parents and grandparents didn't speak openly to children, 'They didn't let us hear what was going on. Now we would like to ask, but our parents and grandparents have died. There it is.' She remembered the blackout:

> We had lamps, no electricity, and you had to keep the lamp low and dim and we always tried to speak in lower tones in case the Germans landed [laughs]. There was a fear of the German U-boats in the water around Barbados and we lived close to the beach.

In 1942 the Canadian ship *Cornwallis* sailed near Barbados Harbour and was torpedoed and sunk by a German U-boat. It was a major incident that made news across the Caribbean. Loleta remembered:

> We didn't have any air raids, but the sinking of the *Cornwallis* near the harbour was the first real incident we had. It was about six o'clock in the evening and I can remember hearing this loud bang and vibration, a blast. We thought maybe the soldiers are practicing. As we lived so near, from the beach, within minutes we heard that the Germans are here, they've bombed a boat. It was very disturbing. Families were advised to stay in their homes until it was safe.

Loleta remembered food rationing:

> We had coupons in alphabetical order so on the day your surname came up you went to places like doctors' surgeries and schools to queue up to get your coupons and that would have given you rations for rice, sugar and things like that. Kerosene was rationed. Rice. Clothing. Your parents would try and be early into the queue.

BBC Radio programmes (aka Rediffusion), relayed by cable into Barbadian homes, kept families in touch with the rest of the world:

Whether you were poor or not, Rediffusion brought us instant news about the war from the BBC's Empire Service in England. We listened to concerts and classical music and on Sundays we could hear a half-hour service from St Martin-in-the-Fields, the church in Trafalgar Square, and we would dream about visiting London one day and going to St Martin-in-the-Fields.

Loleta was familiar with the term 'mother country', 'Yes, the term Mother Country was used because we were part of the British Empire. England was the land of milk and honey and we said it was the Mother Country.'

In 1956 Loleta travelled to London to train as a nurse.

(Loleta Jemmott was interviewed by Stephen Bourne on 20 February 2008.)

Olu Richards (Sierra Leone)

Britain's colonies in West Africa – Gambia, Sierra Leone, the Gold Coast (now Ghana) and Nigeria – all supported the war effort and served as staging posts and military bases. Olu Richards was born in Freetown, the capital city of Sierra Leone and a major port on the Atlantic Ocean in West Africa. He was the son of a mechanical engineer. Olu was 5 years old in 1939 when the Second World War started. He said, 'Sierra Leone was fully involved in the war and lots of soldiers were recruited from Sierra Leone. It was a strategic country. I was told that King George VI visited Freetown on at least one occasion during the war.' Olu remembered air-raid blackouts:

You were not supposed to put your lights on in your houses. Most of these houses were timber and if the security men pass by in the evening and see a light they would come and knock on your door. 'Put out that light! Put out that light!' And most people during the blackout when they did not want people to know they had light they used candles or oil lamps, but security sometimes spy in your house and see the light and come and knock on your door. There was no punishment.

They had air-raid drills at the Christian missionary school that Olu attended:

They told us what to do if you heard the siren or planes flying overhead. It was definitely frightening for a young child. Once or twice I had to lay flat in the gutter when I heard the aeroplane flying above. People panicked when they heard the aeroplanes flying above. They told everybody to have sandbags in their houses and if something suspicious dropped in their house you can just go and put sand over it.

Olu remembered a gun at the east end of Freetown:

It's still there, I think, as a monument, because they call the place Upgun. And there was another gun down at Kingtown which was pointing towards the Atlantic. So we were ready if there was any German planes coming to attack. Local men were trained to man the guns. This was colonial days and the British were in charge of everything and trained the men.

Rediffusion provided families with news of the war:

We didn't have a wireless radio we had Rediffusion. It was wired to the broadcasting station in Freetown, just like electricity wire, standing on poles, and most houses had this. It was a box with one station, the BBC's West Africa service. Mainly news and some music.

Olu recalled that Adolf Hitler was viewed as 'a wicked person' who 'brought disaster to the world'. He said that, after the African

American athlete Jesse Owens did well at the Olympics in 1936, word got back to the people of Freetown that Hitler did not like Owens' success because he was a black man:

> The news got back to us that Hitler would use the skin of a black man to make shoes. People took it very seriously. He was an evil man. They used to nickname a bad person 'Hitler' or 'You're wicked like Hitler' [laughs].

When Olu came to London in 1958 he saw many bomb sites, especially in the East End. He said he saw the results of war.

Independence came to Sierra Leone in 1964. Regarding the term 'mother country', Olu explained:

> Freed slaves were taken to Freetown and although they were in Freetown, they regarded England as their mother country. They were British subjects and so some said they were going back to their mother country. So those liberated Africans who were taken to Freetown in the beginning regarded England as their mother country. The term was still being used when I was growing up.

(Olu Richards was interviewed by Stephen Bourne on 19 February 2008.)

Randol DaCosta (Barbados)

Randol DaCosta was born in Store Gap, near Portadown Hill, in Barbados:

> My father was what we call a hawker. A person that has a donkey cart and he would go to the farm and buy yams and potatoes and things like that and then he'd go round the village and sell them.

Randol was 3 years old when the war started:

> My parents talked about the war, but not to us, but we would
> listen in at the door. There was no electricity in the streets.
> We had lamps and we used kerosene oil to light it. We didn't
> have blackout curtains. My mother used meal bags, flour bags,
> bleach them out and sew them together to block out the win-
> dows. Radios was very scarce. Only a few people could afford
> them. My brother in law used to work in the wharfside, in the
> harbour, and so anything that goes on in the town, he would
> tell us. That's how we heard about the war.

Randol has vivid memories of the German U-boat sinking the
Canadian ship *Cornwallis* in 1942:

> The *Cornwallis* would bring provisions to Barbados, like bully
> beef, cod fish, biscuits. And they bomb it in the harbour.
> Bridgetown harbour. We lived on a hill so you can see the
> whole of Bridgetown. So you hear this big bang and see black
> smoke and everybody wondered what was going on. One of
> my neighbours she came home from work and everybody
> wanted to know what was going on. Then we heard it was
> the *Cornwallis*. They torpedoed it right in the harbour. I didn't
> see the ship myself, but people used to go down to the seaside
> to get the bully beef that wash into shore and carry it home
> because people wanted provisions. Food was short.

Randol said that the sinking of the *Cornwallis* caused some conflict between the British and the Americans:

> The Americans didn't think the British were looking after
> Barbados as they should. So they wanted to come in and secure
> Barbados more. The Americans had their own submarines in
> the harbour, but then the British said this was our island, we
> don't want you to invade it, so that caused an upset between
> the British and the Americans.

At the end of the war, Barbados celebrated, and Randol remembered school ending earlier, 'People beat drums and let off fireworks. So, we knew that the war was finished. I remember a kind of enjoyment.'

Randol was 15 when he left Barbados to join his sister in London. 'My first impression was seeing all these factories, but I never knew they were the chimneys of the houses. I saw bombsites all over the place.' He said that when he was a child England was referred to as the 'mother country':

To my understanding they said the Queen was the mother to all of the West Indies, so I think that's where the term come from. That the Queen is your mother. Because everywhere you go in Barbados there is a photograph of the Queen. But I think mother country came from Queen Victoria, because Barbados was known as Little England. Because everything we were taught at school was English. My best friend in Barbados was white. We were at school together, we eat together, we play together. So I didn't know anything about difference or prejudice until I come to England. I wasn't taught that.

(Randol DaCosta was interviewed by Stephen Bourne on 6 March 2008.)

Cerene Palmer (Jamaica)

Cerene Palmer was born in Whitby District, Manchester, Jamaica. Two of Cerene's uncles, Clinton Ken Enright (her mother's brother) and Joe Palmer (her father's brother) joined the RAF:

I remember going to the post box to look for letters from Uncle Ken who was in the Royal Air Force but, when he came home on leave, he didn't speak about it. I think he had a rough time. He might have been homesick. Many things for black ones were difficult.

Cerene's grandmother, Tammar Palmer, who was born in the Victorian era, died at the age of 98 in the 1970s:

My grandmother used to say, 'I'm going to England', and we say, 'but you don't know anybody there!' [laughs]. She said she don't mind because she is British, and England is the mother country. The term mother country was while slavery was abolished and we became a single British colony, in the British West Indies, and we'd say, 'England is our mother country'. It could have come from Queen Victoria because my grandmother used to refer to her a lot. She was so proud of 'Mrs Queen Victoria'. She used to curtsey every time she referred to 'Mrs Queen Victoria'. During the war she would have been in her sixties so she must have been born when Queen Victoria ruled.

Cerene remembered that evacuees from Kingston, Jamaica, were sent to the rural parts of Jamaica because of the fear of a German invasion. She also remembered rationing:

We had food shortages during the war and one of the things that I remember is sugar. The native people make their own sugar. We'd squeeze the sugar cane to make the juice to get sugar. We know how to make sugar. You have people coming round buying sugar, but somehow it went. It dried up. We couldn't get any sugar anymore and then we had these people come with granulated, white sugar. We had flour. Saltfish. And because we were country people, we had our own produce. We had our own oranges, avocado pears, bread fruit, banana, tangerine, mandarin, satsuma. Anything you can think of, we had. We cultivate our own plot of land. My grandfather was a farmer, and his father before him but, by the time my father and mother come along, they were looking for something better to do. That's why they migrate from the country to the town area. To make a better life.

Cerene heard about the German boats and submarines in the sea:

... but in those days when adults speak, children were not allowed to listen. And when we hear those things they said, 'Go away'. And some they say no, we have to know because when the plane is bombing, we call them rogue planes, we have to know to run and hide. But we didn't get any rogue planes. We used to hear about U-boat but we didn't think about it because we didn't know what it means. Children were definitely protected from the war.

Cerene remembered the British Commissioner coming to the school building and inviting the whole village, or two or three villages to join him:

He tell us how bad the war was, and what they needed, and what co-operation they needed from us because we used to send oranges and fruits and things. I remember my godmother picking the best oranges for King George and 'Lady Queen Elizabeth'. We used to laugh at that. They needed iron and West Indians used a lot of iron parts. So whoever had iron parts, a spoon, whatever, they sent it. In the town area they probably gave money and knitted socks and balaclavas [for the war effort] but in the country area we gave the food we produced. We were helping the mother country because we were already under that umbrella and one day you might want to come to the mother country.

Cerene said the people of Jamaica didn't want the Germans to invade England as they did France. At that time in Jamaica there was many nationalities. Cerene remembered Germans, Irish,

English, Greek, Chinese and Japanese, 'a whole lot of them. They all pulled together for the war effort. Every last person.' News about the war came from the radio and the theatre:

Every West Indian loved the theatre. Anything to do with art. Acting. Painting. Not every house might have a radio, but everyone's ears were pealed to it. At the theatre we called it the intermission. The intermission would come on and before the film started, the war newsreels would come up on the screen and you'd hear the voice telling you and that's when we know what ships look like, and we see the bombing and people running. The newsreels came on again after the film, before you go out. We were really kept informed.

Hitler and Mussolini were hated:

You don't want to know what we thought of Hitler [laughs]. You'd hear men say, 'You just bring him to me [laughs] and I'll chop him right down the middle!' There was a song in Jamaica, I think it was a calypso, 'Mussolini/You know you're wrong/ Mussolini/Don't be so strong'. Really nice lyrics it have to it. All of a sudden, they'd put it on and let it blast.

Cerene remembered a street celebration at the end of the war:

We waved a branch of a tree and listened to calypsos. The whole island took part. When you find out that all that is not over your head anymore, then you go out and celebrate and, boy, the black person certainly know how to celebrate! [laughs].

In 1964 Cerene travelled to London to train as a nurse.

(Cerene Palmer was interviewed by Stephen Bourne on 10 July 2008.)

Notes

Author's Note

1 'Map of Black Families in London', from a report entitled *Negro Families in Cardiff and London in 1935* by Nancie Hare, quoted in Howard Bloch, 'Black People in Canning Town and Custom House between the Wars', *Black and Asian Studies Association Newsletter* No. 14 (January 1996), p.5. Regrettably the report appears to have been lost. There is no copy in the British Library and the author's efforts to trace the copy seen by Howard Bloch in the Newham Local Studies Library has been unsuccessful.

2 Ian Spencer, 'World War Two and the Making of Multi-Racial Britain', in *War Culture: Social Change and Changing Experience in World War Two*, edited by Pat Kirkham and David Thoms (Lawrence & Wishart, 1995), p. 212.

3 *We Were There: For 200 Years Ethnic Minorities have Fought for Britain All Over the World* (Director General Corporate Communications/Ministry of Defence, 2002), p. 13.

4 Richard Smith, 'Second World War', *The Oxford Companion to Black British History* (Oxford University Press, 2007), pp. 436–37.

Introduction

1 Stephen Bourne, *Speak of Me as I Am: The Black Presence in Southwark Since 1600*, p. 64.

2 Harold Macmillan memorandum, 14 September 1942, Public Record Office, CO 876/14.

3   Ken Follett, *Hornet Flight* (Macmillan, 2002), p. 9.
4   www.ken-follett.com. See also David Brewster, *Trinidad Express*,
    25 January 2004.
5   *Ibid.*
6   *Ibid.*
7   *The Forgotten Volunteers*, BBC Radio 2, 11 November 2000.
8   *Ibid.*
9   'Soldiers of the Crown', *The Black Man in Britain, 1550–1950*, BBC 2,
    6 December 1974.
10 *Ibid.* See also Stephen Bourne, 'Ivor Cummings (1913–1992)', *Oxford
    Dictionary of National Biography* (Oxford University Press) and Dudley
    Thompson, *From Kingston to Kenya: The Making of a Pan-Africanist Lawyer*
    (The Majority Press, 1993).
11 Ray Costello, interviewed by Danielle Weekes in 'War of Words
    (60 Years after D-Day, History Must be Rewritten to Include Tales of
    Black Servicemen)', *The Voice* (31 May 2004), pp. 12–13.

1   3 September 1939

1   Mavis Nicholson, *What Did You Do in the War, Mummy?*, p. 23.
2   *Ibid.*, pp. 23–24.
3   Pauline Henriques, interview with Stephen Bourne, Brighton,
    4 August 1989.
4   Mavis Nicholson, p. 24.
5   Pauline Henriques, interview with Stephen Bourne, Brighton,
    8 March 1995.
6   Stephen Bourne, *Sophisticated Lady: A Celebration of Adelaide Hall*, p. 43.
7   Adelaide Hall, interview with Stephen Bourne, London, 21 July 1993.
8   Stephen Bourne and Esther Bruce, *Esther Bruce: A Black London
    Seamstress*, pp. 15–16.
9   Earl Cameron, interview with Stephen Bourne, London, 2 July 1997.

2   The Colour Bar

1   Roi Ottley, *No Green Pastures: The Negro in Europe Today* (John Murray,
    1952), p. 19.
2   Stephen Bourne, *Black Poppies: Britain's Black Community and the Great War*.
3   *Lest We Forget*, Channel 4, 8 November 1990.
4   *Ibid.*
5   CO323/1692 File 7213/3, Dr Harold Moody to Malcolm MacDonald,
    7 December 1939.
6   Harold Moody, on *Lest We Forget*.

7   *Hear-Say*, BBC 2, 7 August 1990.

8   Hakim Adi, *West Africans in Britain 1900–1960*, p. 91.

9   Lilian Bader, *Wartime Memoirs of a WAAF 1939–1944*, pp. 1–2.

10 Ben Bousquet and Colin Douglas, *West Indian Women at War: British Racism in World War II*, pp. 129–30.

11 *Ibid.*

12 *Parliamentary Debates*, 5th series, Vol. 392 (1943), cols 390–91. See also Peter Fryer, *Staying Power: The History of Black People in Britain*, p. 364.

13 *Ibid.*

14 Peter Ginn, Ruth Goodman and Alex Langlands, *Wartime Farm* (Mitchell Beazley, 2012), pp. 58–61.

3   Dr Harold Moody

1   Edward Scobie, *Black Britannia: A History of Blacks in Britain*, p. 148. See also Stephen Bourne, *Dr Harold Moody* and Sam Morris, 'Moody – The Forgotten Visionary', *New Community*, Vol. 1, No. 3 (Spring 1972), pp. 193–96.

2   League of Coloured Peoples (LCP), *News Letter*, 23 (August 1941), pp. 98–99.

3   *Ibid.*, 10 (July 1940), p. 63.

4   *Ibid.*, 14 (November 1940), p. 25.

5   David A. Vaughan, *Negro Victory: The Life Story of Dr Harold Moody*, p. 117.

6   LCP *News Letter*, 16 (January 1941), p. 102.

7   Cynthia Moody, *Ronald Moody: A Profile* (May 1997), pp. 2–3.

8   *Calling the West Indies*, 1 February 1943, BBC Written Archives.

4   Conscientious Objector

1   'A Negro Recital', *The Times* (7 March 1932), p. 10.

2   LCP *News Letter*, 25 (October 1941), p. 3.

3   *News Letter*, 29 (February 1942), pp. 98–99.

5   Evacuees

1   Ben Wicks, *No Time to Wave Goodbye: The Story of Britain's 3,500,000 Evacuees* (Bloomsbury, 1988), p. 97.

2   *Ibid.*

3   LCP, Letter No. 2, *News Notes* (November 1939), p. 2.

4   Trevor Sawtell, 'Memories of Wartime Evacuees in Ebbw Vale', *WW2 People's War*, www.bbc.co.uk.

5   Howard Bloch, 'Black People in Canning Town and Custom House
    between the Wars', *Black and Asian Studies Association, Newsletter* 14
    (January 1996), p. 5.
6   Anita Bowes, interview with Stephen Bourne, London, 27 January 1996.
7   Christopher Cozier, interview with Stephen Bourne, London,
    1 March 1996.
8   Joseph Cozier, interview with Stephen Bourne, London, 9 March 1996.

6   The Call of the Sea

1   Ray Costello, *Black Liverpool: The Early History of Britain's Oldest Black
    Community 1730–1918*, pp. 53–54.
2   Steve Humphries, 'Sailors at War' in *The Call of the Sea: Britain's Maritime
    Past 1900–1960*, pp. 119.
3   Sid Graham, interviewed by Howard Bloch at the Cundy Centre,
    Hartington Road, Custom House, 7 October 1993. Used with
    Mr Bloch's permission.
4   Sue Elliott and Steve Humphries, *Britain's Greatest Generation*, p. 141.
5   Humphries, *The Call of the Sea*, p. 120.
6   *Ibid.*, 120–21.
7   'All at sea in battle for survival', *The Newham Mag* (VE Day Special),
    7 May 2005.
8   Humphries, *The Call of the Sea*, p. 121.
9   Interview with Howard Bloch, 7 October 1993.

7   The London Blitz

1   Stephen Bourne, *Sophisticated Lady: A Celebration of Adelaide Hall*, p. 44.
2   *Ibid.*
3   Kenny Lynch, interview with Stephen Bourne, London, 24 July 1991.
4   Stephen Bourne and Esther Bruce, *Esther Bruce: A Black London
    Seamstress*, p. 16.
5   Letter to Winston Churchill, 10 October 1941, PRO CO 859 77/1.
6   *Ibid.*
7   Oku Ekpenyon, 'An ARP Man's Story', *BBC History Magazine*,
    1/5 (September 2000), p. 47.
8   E.I. Ekpenyon, *Some Experiences of an African Air Raid Warden*, p. 10.
9   *Ibid.*
10 *Ibid.*, pp. 7–8.
11 A.A. Thompson, 'Coloured People and the London Blitz', LCP *News
    Letter*, 15 (December 1940), pp. 67–68.
12 Fernando Henriques, *Children of Caliban: Miscegenation*, p. 3.

13 Mark Holland (ed.), *The Jippi-Jappa Hat Merchant and His Family: A Jamaican Family in Britain*, pp. 170–72.

14 *Ibid.*

15 Henriques, *Children of Caliban*, p. 3.

16 Fernando Henriques, 'Coloured Men in Civilian Defence', LCP *News Letter* 21 (June 1941), pp. 57–59.

17 Bourne, *Sophisticated Lady*, pp. 43–44.

18 *Ibid.*, p. 44.

19 Bourne and Bruce, p. 23.

20 Stephen Bourne, interview with Esther Bruce, London, 4 July 1990.

21 Joshua Levine, *The Secret History of the Blitz*, pp. 199–200.

22 Bourne and Bruce, pp. 25–26.

23 *Ibid.*, p. 22.

24 *Ibid.*

25 Charles Graves, *Champagne and Chandeliers: The Story of the Café de Paris*, p. 112.

26 *Ibid.*, p. 117.

27 Joe Deniz, interview with Stephen Bourne, London, 10 August 1993.

28 Philip Ziegler, *London at War 1939–1945* (Sinclair-Stevenson, 1995), p. 148.

29 Levine, Joshua, *The Secret History of the Blitz*, p. 255.

30 Angus Calder, *The People's War*, p. 204.

31 Tom Cullen, *The Man who was Norris: The Life of Gerald Hamilton* (Dedalus, 2014), p. 173.

32 Earl Cameron, interviewed by Stephen Bourne, London, 2 July 1997 and Earl Cameron, unpublished autobiography. Used with permission.

8   Liverpool, Cardiff, Manchester and Plymouth

1 *Black Britain (The Mother Country)*, BBC 2, 7 January 1991.

2 'The Cardiff Coloured Mission', LCP *News Letter* 29 (February 1942), p. 110.

3 Kenneth Little, *Negroes in Britain: A Study of Racial Relations in English Society*, pp. 116-17.

4 A.L. Lloyd, *Picture Post*, Vol. 47, No. 4 (22 April 1950), pp. 13–19.

5 John L. Williams, *Miss Shirley Bassey* (Quercus, 2010), pp. 38–39.

6 Michael Herbert, *Never Counted Out! The Story of Len Johnson, Manchester's Black Boxing Hero and Communist*, p. 64. Thanks to Michael Herbert for sharing his correspondence about Len Johnson's wartime experiences.

7 Jonathan Wood, *Bill Miller: Black Labour Party Activist in Plymouth* (History & Social Action Publications, 2006), p. 8.

8   *Ibid.*, p.13.
9   Claude Miller, interview with Stephen Bourne, 22 July 2002.

9   Keeping the Home Fires Burning

1   Elisabeth Welch, interview with Stephen Bourne, London,
    15 August 1993.
2   Charlotte Breese, *Hutch* (Bloomsbury, 1999), p. 165.
3   Richard Fawkes, *Fighting for a Laugh: Entertaining the British and American Armed Forces 1939–1946* (Macdonald and Jane's, 1978), p. 19.
4   Elisabeth Welch, 'A Night to Remember', *Sunday Telegraph*,
    29 November 1992.
5   *Ibid.*
6   Stephen Bourne, *Sophisticated Lady: A Celebration of Adelaide Hall*, p. 45.
7   *Ibid.*
8   *Ibid.*
9   *Ibid.*

10   Ivor Cummings

1   Mike Phillips and Trevor Phillips, *Windrush: The Irresistible Rise of Multi-Racial Britain*, p. 68.
2   Nicholas Boston, 'Ivor Cummings was the Gay Godfather of the Windrush Generation', *The Independent*, 24 June 2019.
3   Mike and Trevor Phillips, p. 84.
4   Memo, Ivor Cummings (Assistant Welfare Officer) to J.L. Keith (Welfare Officer), 19 May 1941, PRO CO 859 76/6.
5   Mike and Trevor Phillips, p. 84.

11   Learie Constantine

1   *Calypso for Constantine*, BBC 1, 16 June 1966.
2   *Ibid.*
3   Gerald Howat, *Learie Constantine*, p. 129.
4   *Calypso for Constantine*, BBC 1, 16 June 1966.
5   Howat, p. 29.
6   Peter Mason, *Learie Constantine*, pp. 78–79.
7   Learie Constantine, *Colour Bar*, pp. 147–48.
8   Peter Mason, *Learie Constantine*, p. 80.
9   *Ibid.*, pp. 81, 83.

10 Memo from G.R. Barnes, director of talks, to Miss Bucknall, 8 July 1943, BBC Written Archives.

11 David Killingray, 'Sir Learie Constantine', *The Oxford Companion to Black British History* (Oxford University Press, 2007), pp. 114–16.

12 'Law Reports' in *The Times*, 20 June, 22 June and 29 June 1944.

13 LCP *News Letter* 58 (July 1944), p. 66.

14 *Calypso for Constantine*, BBC 1, 16 June 1966.

12   The BBC

1   LCP *News Letter* 9 (June 1940), p. 39.

2   Pearl Connor Mogotsi, interviewed by Stephen Bourne, London, 26 July 1993.

3   D.G. Bridson, *Prospero and Ariel – The Rise and Fall of Radio: A Personal Recollection* (Victor Gollancz, 1971), pp. 109–11.

4   Memo from BBC Liaison Officer Mrs Elspeth Huxley to Director of Talks G.R. Barnes, 'Colour Prejudice Discussion', 25 June 1943, and memo from G.R. Barnes to Miss Bucknall, 'Discussion on Colour Prejudice', 30 June 1943, BBC Written Archives. See also Darrell M. Newton, *Paving the Empire Road: BBC Television and Black Britons* (Manchester University Press, 2011), pp. 27–30.

13   Una Marson

1   Delia Jarrett-Macauley, *The Life of Una Marson 1905–1965*, p. 147.

2   'Una Marson joins the BBC staff', *London Calling*, No. 81, 20–26 April 1941, p. 13.

3   Erika Smilowitz, 'Una Marson: Woman Before Her Time', *Jamaica Journal*, Vol. 16, No. 2 (May 1983), pp. 62–68.

4   Delia Jarrett-Macauley, interviewed by Jane Garvey, *Woman's Hour*, BBC Radio 4, 3 March 2009.

5   For further information about *Caribbean Voices*, see Glyne Griffith, 'This is London Calling the West Indies: The BBC's Caribbean Voices', Bill Schwarz (ed.), *West Indian Intellectuals in Britain* (Manchester University Press, 2003).

6   Delia Jarrett-Macauley, *The Life of Una Marson 1905–1965*, p. 160.

7   LCP *News Letter* 67 (April 1945), p. 8.

14   Royal Air Force

1   Mr Fairweather, *We've Come a Long Way* (Golden Oldies Community Care Project, 2019), pp. 16–17.

2 Jim Pines (ed.), *Black and White in Colour: Black People in British Television since 1936* (BFI Publishing, 1992), pp. 43–44.

3 Cy Grant, *'A Member of the RAF of Indeterminate Race': WW2 Experiences of a Former RAF Navigator and POW*, p. 27.

4 Erica Myers-Davis, *Under One Flag: How Indigenous and Ethnic Peoples of the Commonwealth and British Empire Helped Great Britain Win World War II*, pp. 98–99.

5 Sean Douglas, 'World War II Airman Ulric Cross Recalls "The Day I Almost Died"', *Trinidad Express*, 15 November 1999, p. 11.

6 Mike and Trevor Phillips, *Windrush: The Irresistible Rise of Multi-Racial Britain*, pp. 27–29.

7 Valerie Wint, *The Longer Run: A Daughter's Story of Arthur Wint*, p. 42.

8 William Strachan, interviewed by Conrad Wood for the Imperial War Museum, 26 October 1987.

9 E. Martin Noble, *Jamaica Airman: A Black Airman in Britain 1943 and After*, p. 18.

10 Annie Keane, 'Making a Difference – Experiences of a Black British Serviceman', *WW2 People's War*, 2004, www.bbc.co.uk.

11 Roger Lambo, 'Achtung! The Black Prince: West Africans in the Royal Air Force 1939–46', in David Killingray (ed.), *Africans in Britain*, pp. 145–63.

12 *The Times*, 30 January 1945, p. 6.

13 Roy Sloan, *Wings of War over Gwynedd: Aviation in Gwynedd During World War II* (Gwasg Carreg Gwalch, 1991), p. 63.

14 Frank E. Stokes, The Story of an Aircraft Crash Survivor, www.breconbeacons.org

15   Prisoners of War

1 Gemma Romain, *Race, Sexuality and Identity in Britain and Jamaica: The Biography of Patrick Nelson, 1916–1963* (Bloomsbury Academic, 2017).

2 See Cy Grant, *'A Member of the RAF of Indeterminate Race': WW2 Experiences of a Former RAF Navigator and POW*.

3 Jim Pines (ed.), *Black and White in Colour: Black People in British Television since 1936* (BFI Publishing, 1992), pp.43–44.

4 Alec Lom, 'The men of bomber command: the navigator, Cy Grant', *The Telegraph*, 24 October 2008.

5 *Ibid.*

6 *The Forgotten Volunteers*, BBC Radio 2, 11 November 2000.

7 Pines, *Black and White in Colour*, p. 44.

8 Alec Lom, 'The men of bomber command: the navigator, Cy Grant', *The Telegraph*, 24 October 2008.

9   *Ibid*.

10 Pines, *Black and White in Colour*, p. 44.

11 Martin Plaut, 'The Africans who fought in WWII', BBC News, www.bbc.co.uk

12 'African Participants in the Second World War', Memorial Gates Trust, www.mgtrust.org

13 Michael Butscher, 'A Veteran with Attitude', *The Voice*, 9 May 1995, pp. 15–16.

14 'African Participants in the Second World War', Memorial Gates Trust, www.mgtrust.org

15 Butscher, 'A Veteran with Attitude'.

16   Lilian and Ramsay Bader

1   Lilian Bader, *Lilian Bader: Wartime Memoirs of a WAAF 1939–1944*, p. 5.

2   Ben Bousquet and Colin Douglas, *West Indian Women at War: British Racism in World War II*, p. 134.

3   *Lilian Bader: Wartime Memoirs*, p. 9.

4   *Ibid*., pp. 11–12.

5   Ramsay Bader, interviewed by Conrad Wood, Imperial War Museum, 15 January 1989.

6   *Ibid*.

7   *Ibid*.

8   *Ibid*.

9   *The Forgotten Volunteers*, BBC Radio 2, 11 November 2000.

10 Imperial War Museum, 15 January 1989.

11 Benjamin MacRae interviewed by Conrad Wood, Imperial War Museum, 24 February 1989.

17   Auxiliary Territorial Service

1   Joanne Buggins, 'West Indians in Britain during the Second World War: a short history drawing on Colonial Office papers', *Imperial War Museum Review No. 5* (Imperial War Museum, 1990), pp. 93–94.

2   *The Forgotten Volunteers*, BBC Radio 2, 11 November 2000.

3   Nadia Cattouse, interview with Stephen Bourne, London, 8 August 1989.

4   *Ibid*.

5   Nadia Cattouse, *Lest We Forget*, Channel 4, 8 November 1990.

6   Angelina Osborne and Arthur Torrington, *We Served: The Untold Story of the West Indian Contribution to World War II*, p. 9.

7   Norma Best, interviewed by Toby Brooks, Imperial War Museum, 11 October 2007.

8   *Speaking Out and Standing Firm* (documentary film) (2010).

9   Christopher Somerville, *Our War: How the British Commonwealth Fought the Second World War*, pp. 173–74.

10 Ethnic Communities Oral History Project, *The Motherland Calls: African Caribbean Experiences*, p. 1.

11 Osborne and Torrington, *We Served*, p. 17.

12 Oliver Marshall, *The Caribbean at War: British West Indians in World War II*, p.4.

13 Osborne and Torrington, *We Served*, p. 17.

14 *Ibid.*

15 Marshall, *The Caribbean at War*, p. 19.

16 *Ibid.*, p. 24.

18   'They'll Bleed and Suffer and Die': African American GIs in Britain

1   'Marc Blitzstein, Roland Hayes and the "Negro Chorus" at the Royal Albert Hall in 1943', Another Nickel in the Machine, www.nickelinthemachine.com

2   Juliet Gardiner, '*Over Here': The GIs in Wartime Britain*, p. 150.

3   *Ibid.*, p.154.

4   *Ibid.*

5   David Reynolds, *Rich Relations: The American Occupation of Britain, 1942–1945*, p. 303.

6   Philip Ziegler, *London at War 1939–1945*, p. 218.

7   Jack Artis, 'My Black Uncle', *WW2 People's War*, www.bbc.co.uk

8   *The Invisible Force*, BBC Radio 4, 16 May 1989.

9   Neil A. Wynn, "Race War": Black American GIs and West Indians in Britain during the Second World War,' *Immigrants and Minorities*, Vol. 24, No. 3, November 2006, pp. 333–34.

10 Reynolds, *Rich Relations*, p. 307.

11 Wynn, *Race War*, pp.338–39.

12 Phillip McGuire, *Taps for a Jim Crow Army: Letters from Black Soldiers in World War II*, pp. 228–29.

13 Juliet Gardiner, *Wartime: Britain 1939–1945*, p. 484.

19   'A Shameful Business': The Case of George Roberts

1   Carlton Wilson, 'Liverpool's Black Population During World War II', *Black and Asian Studies Newsletter*, 20 (January 1998), pp. 14–15.

2   *Guardian*, 2 August 1944 and LCP *News Letter* 60 (September 1944, pp. 93–94.

3   LCP *News Letter* 71 (August 1945), p. 108.

20   Flying Bombs

1   Juliet Gardiner, *Wartime: Britain 1939–1945*, p. 548.

2   Mavis Nicholson, *What Did You Do in the War, Mummy?*, p. 30.

3   Mark Holland (ed.), *The Jippi-Jappa Hat Merchant and His Family: A Jamaican Family in Britain*, p. 127.

4   Roi Ottley, *Roi Ottley's World War II: The Lost Diary of an African American Journalist*, Mark A. Huddle (ed.), p. 52

5   Stephen Bourne and Esther Bruce, *Esther Bruce: A Black London Seamstress*, p. 24.

6   Leslie Harker, *Fulham in the Second World War* (Fulham and Hammersmith Historical Society, 1984), p. 80.

7   Bourne and Bruce, p. 24.

8   Metropolitan Borough of Fulham Incident List, 2 August 1944.

9   *Wartime: Britain 1939–1945*, p. 560.

10   Roi Ottley, *Roi Ottley's World War II*, p. 132.

11   Edric Connor, *Horizons: The Life and Times of Edric Connor* (Ian Randle, 2007), p. 64.

12   Norman Longmate, *Hitler's Rockets: The Story of the V-2s* (Hutchinson, 1985), p. 208.

13   For further information see Bob Ogley, *Doodlebugs and Rockets: The Battle of the Flying Bombs* (Froglets Publications, 1992), p. 164.

21   Front-Line Films

1   Marie Seton, *Paul Robeson*, p. 78.

2   Paul Robeson Jr, *The Undiscovered Paul Robeson: An Artist's Journey, 1898–1939*, pp. 330–31.

3   Thorold Dickinson, 'Making a film in Tanganyika territory', *British Film Yearbook 1947–48* (British Yearbooks, 1948), p. 53.

4   Marc Matera, *Black London: The Imperial Metropolis and Decolonization in the Twentieth Century*, p. 308.

5   Graham Smith, *When Jim Crow Met John Bull*, p. 88.

6 George Pearson, *Flashback: The Autobiography of a Film-Maker* (George Allen and Unwin, 1957), p. 204.

7 *Colonial Cinema* (1944) 2, 1, p. 3.

22 Mother Country

1 Stephen Bourne and Sav Kyriacou, *A Ship and a Prayer* (ECOHP, 1999), p. 21.

2 Stephen Bourne, *Speak of me as I am*, p. 64.

3 Austin Clarke, *Growing Up Stupid Under the Union Jack: A Memoir*, p. 49.

4 Norman Beaton, *Beaton But Unbowed: An Autobiography* (Methuen, 1986), p. 35.

5 Clarke, *Growing Up Stupid*, pp. 95–96.

6 *Ibid.*

7 Dr Harold Moody, LCP *News Letter* 12 (September 1940).

23 VE Day

1 Stephen Bourne, *Sophisticated Lady: A Celebration of Adelaide Hall*, p. 45.

2 *Birthrights*, BBC 2, 5 July 1993.

3 *The Forgotten Volunteers*, BBC Radio 2, 11 November 2000.

4 Angelina Osborne and Arthur Torrington, *We Served*, p. 19.

5 Cerene Palmer, interview with Stephen Bourne, London, 10 July 2008.

6 *The Invisible Force*, BBC Radio 4, 16 May 1989.

7 Angelina Osborne and Arthur Torrington, *We Served*, p. 23.

8 E. Martin Noble, *Jamaica Airman: A Black Airman in Britain 1943 and After*, p. 53.

9 *A Charmed Life* (documentary film) (2009).

10 Edric Connor, *Horizons: The Life and Times of Edric Connor*, p. 65.

11 Marc Matera, *Black London: The Imperial Metropolis and Decolonization in the Twentieth Century*, p. 179.

12 *Ibid.*

13 'Calling the West Indies', LCP *News Letter* 69 (June 1945), p. 48.

14 David A. Vaughan, *Negro Victory: The Life Story of Dr Harold Moody*, p. 55 and Sam Morris, 'Moody – the Forgotten Visionary', *New Community*, Vol. 1, No. 3, Spring, 1972. Note: The LCP continued campaigning for several years after Dr Moody died, but went into decline at the time of the post-war increase of African and Caribbean settlers in Britain; they could have benefited from an organisation that represented their interests and campaigned on their behalf. In 1995 an English Heritage Blue Plaque was erected on Dr Moody's Peckham home, 164 Queen's

Road, and in 2009 Ronald Moody's 1946 bronze portrait of his brother was put on permanent display in Peckham Library.

15   Mavis Nicholson, *What Did You Do in the War, Mummy?* (Chatto & Windus, 1995), p. 30.

16   *Black Britain (The Mother Country)*, BBC 2, 7 January 1991.

17   'Rhythm in Berlin', *Time*, 10 September 1945.

24   If Hitler Had Invaded

1   'The Forgotten Black Victims of Nazi Germany – What Hitler Did to the Races he Deemed "Inferior"', *The Voice* (16–22 February 2009), pp. 16–17.

2   Norman Longmate, letter to Stephen Bourne, 23 February 2006.

3   *Hear-Say*, BBC 2, 7 August 1990.

Further Reading

Adi, Hakim, *West Africans in Britain 1900–1960* (Lawrence & Wishart, 1998).

Bader, Lilian, *Lilian Bader: Wartime Memoirs of a WAAF 1939–1944* (Imperial War Museum, 1989).

Beula, Jak, and Nairobi Thompson (eds), *Remembered – In Memoriam: An Anthology of African and Caribbean Experiences WW1 and WW2* (Nu Jak Media Publishing, 2017).

Bourne, Stephen, *Sophisticated Lady: A Celebration of Adelaide Hall* (ECOHP, 2001).

Bourne, Stephen, *Speak of Me as I Am: The Black Presence in Southwark Since 1600* (Southwark Council, 2005).

Bourne, Stephen, *Dr Harold Moody* (Southwark Council, 2008).

Bourne, Stephen, *Black Poppies: Britain's Black Community and the Great War* (The History Press, 2019).

Bourne, Stephen, and Esther Bruce, *Esther Bruce: A Black London Seamstress* (History & Social Action Publications).

Bousquet, Ben, and Colin Douglas, *West Indian Women at War: British Racism in World War II* (Lawrence & Wishart, 1991).

Calder, Angus, *The People's War* (Jonathan Cape, 1969).

Clarke, Austin, *Growing Up Stupid Under the Union Jack: A Memoir* (Ian Randle, 2003).

Connor, Edric, *Horizons: The Life and Times of Edric Connor* (Ian Randle, 2007).

Constantine, Learie, *Colour Bar* (Stanley Paul, 1954).

Costello, Ray, *Black Liverpool: The Early History of Britain's Oldest Black Community 1730–1918* (Picton Press, 2001).

Cullen, Tom, *The Man who was Norris: The Life of Gerald Hamilton* (Dedalus, 2014).

Dabydeen, David, Gilmore, John, and Cecily Jones (eds), *The Oxford Companion to Black British History* (Oxford University Press, 2007).

Ekpenyon, E.I., *Some Experiences of an African Air Raid Warden* (The Sheldon Press, 1943).

Elliott, Sue, and Steve Humphries, *Britain's Greatest Generation: How Our Parents and Grandparents Made the Twentieth Century* (Random House, 2015).

Ethnic Communities Oral History Project, *The Motherland Calls: African Caribbean Experiences* (Hammersmith and Fulham Community History Series No. 4/ECOHP, 1989).

Ford, Amos A., *Telling the Truth: The Life and Times of the British Honduran Forestry Unit in Scotland (1941–44)* (Karia Press, 1985).

Fryer, Peter, *Staying Power: The History of Black People in Britain* (Pluto, 1984).

Gardiner, Juliet, '*Over Here': The GIs in Wartime Britain* (Collins and Brown, 1992).

Gardiner, Juliet, *Wartime: Britain 1939–1945* (Headline, 2004).

Gardiner, Juliet, *The Blitz: The British Under Attack* (HarperPress, 2010).

Grant, Cy, *'A Member of the RAF of Indeterminate Race': WW2 Experiences of a Former RAF Navigator and POW* (Woodfield Publishing, 2006).

Graves, Charles, *Champagne and Chandeliers: The Story of the Café de Paris* (Odhams Press, 1958).

Heaton, Louis, 'For King and Country', *The Voice* (12 November 1983, pp. 16–17).

Henriques, Fernando, *Children of Caliban: Miscegenation* (Secker and Warburg, 1974).

Herbert, Michael, *Never Counted Out! The Story of Len Johnson, Manchester's Black Boxing Hero and Communist* (Dropped Aitches Press, 1992).

Holland, Mark (ed.), *The Jippi-Jappa Hat Merchant and His Family: A Jamaican Family in Britain* (Horsgate, 2014).

Howat, Gerald, *Learie Constantine* (George Allen and Unwin, 1975).

Huddle, Mark A. (ed.), *Roi Ottley's World War II: The Lost Diary of an African American Journalist* (University Press of Kansas, 2011).

Humphries, Steve, *The Call of the Sea: Britain's Maritime Past 1900–1960* (BBC Books, 1997).

Imperial War Museum, '"Together": A Multi-Media Resource Pack on the Contribution Made in the Second World War by African, Asian and Caribbean Men and Women' (1995).

Jackson, Robert, *The London Blitz* (Museum of London, 1990).

Jarrett-Macauley, Delia, *The Life of Una Marson 1905–1965* (Manchester University Press, 1998).

Killingray, David, *Fighting for Britain: African Soldiers in the Second World War* (James Currey, 2010).

Lambo, Roger, 'Achtung! The Black Prince: West Africans in the Royal Air Force 1939–46', in David Killingray (ed.), *Africans in Britain* (Frank Cass, 1994).

Levine, Joshua, *The Secret History of the Blitz* (Simon and Schuster, 2015).

Little, Kenneth, *Negroes in Britain: A Study in Racial Relations in English Society* (Kegan Paul, 1948).

Lusane, Clarence, *Hitler's Black Victims: The Historical Experiences of Afro-Germans, European Blacks, Africans, and African Americans in the Nazi Era* (Routledge, 2002).

McGuire, Phillip, *Taps for a Jim Crow Army: Letters from Black Soldiers in World War II* (ABC-Clio, 1983).

Marshall, Oliver, *The Caribbean at War: British West Indians in World War II* (The North Kensington Archive, 1992).

Mason, Peter, *Learie Constantine* (Signal Books, 2008).

Matera, Marc, *Black London: The Imperial Metropolis and Decolonisation in the Twentieth Century* (University of California Press, 2015).

Murray, Robert. N., *Lest We Forget: The Experiences of World War II West Indian Ex-Service Personnel* (Nottingham West Indian Combined Ex-Services Association/Hansib, 1996).

Myers-Davis, Erica, *Under One Flag: How Indigenous and Ethnic Peoples of the Commonwealth and British Empire Helped Great Britain Win World War II* (Get Publishing, 2009).

Nicholson, Mavis, *What Did You Do in the War, Mummy?* (Chatto & Windus, 1995).

Noble, E. Martin, *Jamaica Airman: A Black Airman in Britain 1943 and After* (New Beacon Books, 1984).

Notting Dale Urban Studies Centre and Ethnic Communities Oral History Project, *Sorry No Vacancies: Life Stories of Senior Citizens From the Caribbean* (Notting Dale Urban Studies Centre/ECOHP, 1992).

Olusoga, David, *Black and British: A Forgotten History* (Macmillan, 2016).

Osborne, Angelina, and Arthur Torrington, *We Served: The Untold Story of the West Indian Contribution to World War II* (Krik Krak, 2005).

Ottley, Roi, *Roi Ottley's World War II: The Lost Diary of an African American Journalist*, edited by Mark A. Huddle, (University Press of Kansas, 2011).

Phillips, Mike and Trevor Phillips, *Windrush: The Irresistible Rise of Multi-Racial Britain* (HarperCollins, 1998).

Pines, Jim (ed.), *Black and White in Colour: Black People in British Television Since 1936* (BFI Publishing, 1992).

Reynolds, David, *Rich Relations: The American Occupation of Britain, 1942–1945* (HarperCollins, 1995).

Robeson Jr, Paul, *The Undiscovered Paul Robeson: An Artist's Journey, 1898–1939* (John Wiley & Sons, 2001).

Schwarz, Bill (ed.), *West Indian Intellectuals in Britain* (Manchester University Press, 2003).

Scobie, Edward, *Black Britannia: A History of Blacks in Britain* (Johnson Publishing Company, 1972).

Seton, Marie, *Paul Robeson* (Dennis Dobson, 1958).

Sherwood, Marika, *Many Struggles: West Indian Workers and Service Personnel in Britain 1939–1945* (Karia Press, 1985).

Sherwood, Marika, *World War II: Colonies and Colonials* (Savannah Press, 2013).

Smith, Graham, *When Jim Crow Met John Bull: Black American Soldiers in World War II Britain* (I.B. Tauris, 1987).

Somerville, Christopher, *Our War: How the British Commonwealth Fought the Second World War* (Weidenfeld & Nicolson, 1998).

Thompson, Dudley, *From Kingston to Kenya: The Making of a Pan-Africanist Lawyer* (The Majority Press, 1993).

Vaughan, David A., *Negro Victory: The Life Story of Dr Harold Moody* (Independent Press, 1950).

Webster, Wendy, *Englishness and Empire 1939–1965* (Oxford University Press, 2005).

Wint, Valerie, *The Longer Run: A Daughter's Story of Arthur Wint* (Ian Randle, 2012).

Ziegler, Philip, *London at War 1939–1945* (Sinclair-Stevenson, 1995).

For further information about the following black Britons who are featured in *Under Fire*, please refer to the *Oxford Dictionary of National Biography* (www.oxforddnb.com). Listed by author they are:

Hakim Adi

Paul Robeson (1898–1976)

Stephen Bourne

Robert Adams (1900–65)
Lilian Bader (1918–2015)
Esther Bruce (1912–94)
Edric Connor (1913–68)
Ulric Cross (1917–2003)
Ivor Cummings (1913–92)
Reginald Foresythe (1907–58)
Cy Grant (1919–2010)
Adelaide Hall (1901–93)
Fernando Henriques (1916–76)

Pauline Henriques (1914–98)
Leslie 'Hutch' Hutchinson (1900–69)
Sam King (1926–2016)
Connie Mark (1923–2007)
Orlando Martins (1899–1985)
John Payne (1872–1952)
George A. Roberts (1891–1970)
Peter Thomas (1914–45)
Elisabeth Welch (1904–2003)

Denise deCaires Narain

Una Marson (1905–65)

Peter D. Fraser

William 'Billy' Strachan (1921–98)

Gerald M.D. Howat

Learie Constantine (1901–71)

David Killingray

Dr Harold Moody (1882–1947)

Howard Rye

Rudolph Dunbar (1899–1988)

Marika Sherwood

Daniels Ekarte (1896/97–1964)

Val Wilmer

Ambrose Campbell (1919–2006)
Joe Deniz (1913–94)
Ken 'Snakehips' Johnson (1914–41)

About the Author

Stephen Bourne is a writer, film and social historian specialising in black heritage and gay culture. Bonnie Greer, the acclaimed playwright and critic, said, 'Stephen brings great natural scholarship and passion to a largely hidden story. He is highly accessible, accurate and surprising. You always walk away from his work knowing something that you didn't know, that you didn't even expect.'

Stephen graduated from the London College of Printing with a bachelor's degree in film and television in 1988, and in 2006 received a Master of Philosophy degree at De Montfort University for his dissertation on the subject of the representation of gay men in British television drama. In 2017, he was awarded an Honorary Fellowship by London South Bank University for his contribution to diversity.

From 1989, Stephen was a research officer at the British Film Institute on a project that documented the history of black people in British television. The result was a two-part television documentary called *Black and White in Colour* (BBC 2, 1992) that is considered ground breaking. In 1991, Stephen was a founder member of the Black and Asian Studies Association. In the 1990s, he undertook pioneering work with Southwark Council and the Metropolitan Police that resulted in the founding of one of the first locally based LGBT forums to address homophobic and transphobic crime.

Since 1999 he has been a voluntary independent adviser to the police. In 2002, Stephen received the Metropolitan Police Volunteer Award 'in recognition of dedicated service and commitment to supporting the Metropolitan Police in Southwark', and in 2020 Southwark Police presented Stephen with a commendation for twenty years' public service as an independent advisor.

In 1991, Stephen co-authored *Aunt Esther's Story* with Esther Bruce (his adopted aunt), which was published by Hammersmith and Fulham's Ethnic Communities Oral History. In 2008, he researched *Keep Smiling Through: Black Londoners on the Home Front, 1939–1945*, an exhibition for the Cuming Museum in the London Borough of Southwark, and that same year he was a historical consultant on the Imperial War Museum's 'From War to Windrush' exhibition.

In 2014, Stephen's first edition of *Black Poppies: Britain's Black Community and the Great War* was published by The History Press to coincide with the centenary of Britain's entry into the First World War. For *Black Poppies*, Stephen received the 2015 Southwark Arts Forum Literature Award. An updated edition of *Black Poppies* was published in 2019.

In 2016, Stephen's acclaimed biography of the singer Evelyn Dove, *Evelyn Dove: Britain's Black Cabaret Queen*, was published by Jacaranda Books. In 2017 came *Fighting Proud: The Untold Story of the Gay Men who Served in Two World Wars* for I.B. Tauris, and in 2018, *War to Windrush: Black Women in Britain 1939–1948* for Jacaranda Books.

In 2017, Stephen was honoured by Screen Nation with a special award for documenting black British film and television heritage. In 2019, he curated *Forgotten Black TV Drama*, a retrospective for BFI Southbank and, later that year, Stephen's *Playing Gay in the Golden Age of British TV* was published by The History Press.

For further information go to www.stephenbourne.co.uk

Index

People

Adams, Major Charity 180
Adams, Robert 57, 120, 122, 194, 197
Ademola, Princess 136
Adi, Hakim 9
Alakija, Aduke 122
Alakija, Babatunde O. 148
Aldridge, Amanda Ira 121
Aldridge, Ira 121
Artis, Jack 175
Azikiwe, Nnamdi 197

Bader, Lilian (née Bailey) 52, 68, 159–63, 165
Bader, Ramsay 159–63
Bailey, James 68
Bailey, Lilian *see* Lilian Bader
Baker, Baron 177–8, 209
Baker, Josephine 119
Bassey, Shirley 98
Beaton, Norman 201
Beginner, Lord 200
Benjamin, Louise 98
Beresford, Randolph 199
Best, Norma 166–8, 204

Beula, Jak 21
Blitzstein, Marc 121
Boi, Ransford 151
Bousquet, Ben 16, 165–6
Bovell, Edward 97–8
Bowes, Anita 66
Bruce, Esther 11, 44–5, 76–7, 85–7, 187–8, 209–10
Bruce, Joseph 43–4, 76, 86–7
Buckle, Desmond 57

Calder, Angus 11, 90
Cameron, Earl 45–6, 92–5
Campbell, Ambrose 207
Cattouse, Nadia 166
Chamberlain, Neville 41, 46
Churchill, Winston 14–15, 46, 77, 95–6, 140–1, 146, 175, 203, 206
Clarke, Austin 200–2
Clarke, Dr Cecil Belfield 57, 91–2
Coleridge-Taylor, Avril 121
Coleridge-Taylor, Samuel 121
Connor, Edric 119–20, 189–90, 206–7
Connor, Pearl 119
Constantine, Learie 112–17, 137, 179, 183, 196, 198

Films